TWAYNE'S WORLD AUTHORS SERIES

A Survey of the World's Literature

Sylvia E. Bowman, Indiana University
GENERAL EDITOR

SWEDEN

Leif Sjöberg
State University of New York at Stony Brook
EDITOR

Lars Ahlin

TWAS 430

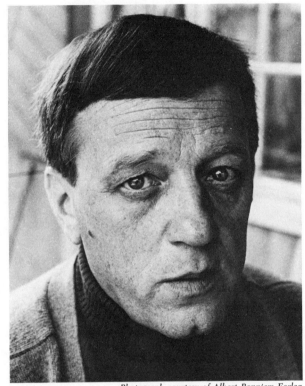

Photograph courtesy of Albert Bonniers Forlag

Lars Ahlin

LARS AHLIN

By TORBORG LUNDELL
University of California at Santa Barbara

TWAYNE PUBLISHERS
A DIVISION OF G. K. HALL & CO., BOSTON

154449

Library of Congress Cataloging in Publication Data

Lundell, Torborg.
  Lars Ahlin.

  (Twayne's world authors series)
  Bibliography: p. 157 - 62.
  Includes index.
  1. Ahlin, Lars Gustav, 1915- — Criticism
and interpretation.
PT9875.A33Z76   839.7'3'72   76-40314
ISBN 0-8057-6270-1

Contents

About the Author

Preface

Acknowledgments

Chronology

1. Development of the Writer   15

2. *Tåbb with the Manifesto*   30

3. Death and Failure   43

4. Failure of Values   74

5. *The Great Amnesia*   94

6. Four Novels on Love   109

7. The Short Stories   140

8. Equality — A Conclusion   144

    Notes and References   147

    Selected Bibliography   157

    Index   163

About the Author

Torborg Louisa Lundell was born in Stockholm, Sweden, and attended the University of Stockholm where she graduated with a fil. mag. (M.A.) in Literature and Political Science in 1964. In 1965 she moved to California and entered graduate school at the University of California, Berkeley. There she studied literary theory and criticism, focusing on modern Swedish and American literature, and received her Ph. D. in Comparative Literature in 1973. She has published articles on Lars Ahlin in American, British, and Swedish professional journals. She has also contributed articles to *The Columbia Dictionary of Modern Literature* on Lars Ahlin, Jan Fridegård, Ivar Lo-Johansson, and Moa Martinson. As the American authority on Lars Ahlin she has been invited to national conferences to present papers dealing with his work. In addition to research activities, she has documented her interest in teaching by writing textbooks in Swedish language and grammar. She is currently teaching Scandinavian and comparative literature, Swedish film and Swedish language at the University of California at Santa Barbara.

Preface

Lars Ahlin is one of Sweden's greatest storytellers. This talent, combined with his incessant interest in aesthetics, has made his writing uniquely intricate and entertaining. While scholarly interest in his work has been growing rapidly in the last ten years, little research has appeared in English and no full-length book has attempted a comprehensive discussion of Ahlin's major ideas. I have kept the bibliographical information to a minimum in order to use more of the allotted space for discussion of the works themselves. Quotations from Ahlin's work and other Swedish sources are my own translations.

In this monograph I have chosen to deal with how death and love, the two main motifs in Ahlin's work, clarify and explain Ahlin's philosophy of equality, the ultimate theme of his novels. Though these motifs are present from Ahlin's earliest to his latest novels, I perceive a shift of focus taking place in his eighth novel, *Stora glömskan (The Great Amnesia, 1954)*. Before this work, Ahlin focuses upon facets of death and failure, with love existing as a redeeming factor. In his later novels Ahlin explores the many facets of love and its superiority over socially created senses of value.

Ahlin's concepts of death and love are based upon theological principles derived primarily from Luther, Barth, Nygren, and other Lutheran theologians. These ideas are presented in the introductions to Chapter 3 (about death and failure) and Chapter 6 (about love), to provide a frame of reference for the novels discussed in Chapters 3, 4, and 6. In a short concluding chapter I summarize his concepts of death and love as they relate to equality in man's sociopsychological concept of self.

From the standpoint of form Ahlin's novels are at the same time stories, and philosophical, theological, and aesthetic manifestos. They are intriguing in their narrative structure which is both complex and innovative, combining features from a variety of literary sources. His interest in the aesthetics of the novel grew out of his early readings of Thomas Mann, André Gide, and Dostoevski, and he was also inspired by the Swedish writer Eyvind Johnson, who spent his formative years in Germany and France in the 1920s. The early Pär Lagerkvist also belongs to the writers Ahlin counts among his important reading experiences.

Furthermore, Ahlin combines the imagination of characterization found in Faulkner and Steinbeck with the playfulness of grammar and language reminiscent of Joyce. Ahlin's narrative attitude is a paradoxical mixture of a Hemingway's detachment and a Saroyan's compassion.

Though he was advised in the beginning to tell his marvelous stories and tales without disturbing experiments in new forms, Ahlin has never ceased searching for new methods of artistic expression. He began to discuss the need for a rejuvenation of the novel in essays from the 1940s, and he has continued his discussions in the novels themselves, as well as in articles and finally in a series of radio speeches in the mid-1960s. He thereby stands as the most important theorist in modern Swedish literature and is largely responsible for the change in artistic consciousness that took place in Swedish letters in the 1950s.

After an introductory chapter I have devoted one chapter to Ahlin's first novel, *Tåbb med Manifestet* (*Tåbb with the Manifesto*, 1943), because of its significance for our understanding of the nature of the conflict between ideals and self in Ahlin's work. I have briefly dealt with his concept of aesthetics in the first chapter, and carried the discussion further in Chapter 4 in connection with his most experimental novel *Om* (*If, About, Around*, 1946). His theory of the function of the writer is also discussed in Chapter 6 in connection with two novels: *Natt i marknadstältet* (*Night in the Market Tent*, 1957) and *Bark och löv* (*Bark and Leaves*, 1961) which most clearly demonstrate his viewpoint.

Innovations in word usage and word formation are other aspects of Ahlin's experiments with artistic communication. I provide examples of these aesthetic features in my discussion of *Om* (*If, About, Around*) in Chapter 4 and *Stora glömskan* (*The Great Amnesia*) in Chapter 5, as well as in *Kvinna kvinna* (*Woman Woman*, 1955) and *Gilla gång* (*Normal Course*, 1958) in Chapter 6.

I have replaced conventional plot summaries, normally required by the Twayne series, with plot analyses, emphasizing those perspectives of the novel which support my discussion of his major motifs. This method is in keeping with Ahlin's intention as a writer; that is, his primary concern is to create a dialogue between the reader and writer which takes place when the reader responds to the text by analyzing it. He therefore often refrains from providing continuity of narration in the conventional sense. This the reader must create for himself; thus, plot summary naturally becomes plot analysis. It is intellectual participation, not merely emotional excitement that Ahlin asks of his readers.

Considering Ahlin's important and exciting production, it is surprising that only two of his short stories have yet been translated into English. Publishers in other languages have been more foresighted: aside from the Scandinavian languages, Ahlin has been translated into French, Slovak, Polish, Czech, and German. Hopefully this monograph will serve as an impetus to make available to the English speaking audience the major works of a writer who is certain to interest and stimulate his readers. I have here tried to present the most important aspects of the many facets in Ahlin's work, and I hope this will be a useful introduction to the writings of one of the most significant authors in modern Swedish literature.

TORBORG LUNDELL

University of California at Santa Barbara

Acknowledgments

I wish to thank the University of California at Santa Barbara for granting a Summer Faculty Fellowship and the Academic Senate for providing a travel grant which enabled me to visit Sweden and collect materials for this study. The visit also gave me the opportunity to make contacts valuable in the preparation of this book.

My most sincere thanks go to Lars Ahlin for reading the manuscript and giving his support and encouragement. I was also fortunate to meet with Filosofie doktor Hans-Göran Ekman who kindly shared his knowledge with me and read my manuscript, contributing invaluable criticism. I am also grateful to Filosofie licentiat Gunde Fredriksson for giving me access to his unpublished thesis.

Furthermore, I want to thank my colleagues Drs. Anthony Mulac and Harry Steinhauer for suggesting stylistic revisions and Professor Leif Sjöberg for editing my manuscript. Remaining flaws of style are, of course, my own responsibility. Finally, my thanks go to Ms. Phyllis Grifman for her patient typing of the manuscript in its different stages of completion.

Chronology

1915   Lars Ahlin born April 4, in Sundsvall, the youngest of seven children.
1918   Family moves to Stockholm.
1920   Parents divorced; children live alone in a sibling community.
1922   Father and children move back to Sundsvall; father remarries.
1928   Leaves school to help support the family. Becomes a member of a Communist youth organization with Ivar Öhman.
1932   Employed at the newspaper *Norrlands-Kuriren*.
1933   Leaves the Communist youth organization and Sundsvall. Has a "mystical experience," a form of hallucinatory vision about the essence of existence. Enters Ålsta folk high school. Meets Arne Jones, a sculptor-to-be.
1934   Writes a review of Ortega y Gasset's *Revolt of the Masses* for school yearbook. Travels with Arne Jones in the summer in door-to-door selling of a poem.
1935   Sets up a book bindery with Arne Jones, which soon fails.
1936   Moves to Stockholm with Arne Jones. Nominated to become a novice in the Societas Sanctae Birgittae.
1937   Finishes his first unpublished novel, *Lille Prometheus (Little Prometheus)*.
1938   Attends Birkagården's folk high school.
1939 -   Finishes his second unpublished novel, *Underklassare av*
1940   *blodet (Of Working Class Blood)*. Hardship period, earning bare subsistence on miscellaneous jobs while unsuccessfully attempting to get published.
1941   Attends the Fjellstedtska school in Uppsala. Received as a member of Societas Sanctae Birgittae.
1942   Drafted to serve his compulsory military service.
1943   Publishes *Tåbb med manifestet (Tåbb with the Manifesto)*.

1944   *Inga ögon väntar mig (No Eyes Await Me).*

1945   "Om ordkonstens kris" ("About the Crisis of the Art of Words") and "Reflexioner and utkast" ("Reflections and Outlines").
        Min död är min (My Death is My Own).

1946   *Om (If, About, Around).* Marries Gunnel Hammar, a writer-to-be.

1947   *Jungfrun i det gröna (Nigella Damascena)* and *Fångnas glädje (Joy of the Imprisoned).*

1948   Publishes *Egen spis (A Stove of One's Own); Lekpaus (Break in the Game)* performed at the Royal Dramatic Theater.

1949   Publishes *Huset har ingen filial (The House Has No Annex); Eld av eld (Fire from Fire)* performed on Swedish Radio.

1950   Publishes *Eld av eld (Fire from Fire).*

1952   Publishes *Fromma mord (Pious Murders).*

1953   Publishes *Kanelbiten (Cinnamon Girl).*

1954   Publishes *Stora glömskan (The Great Amnesia).*

1955   Publishes *Kvinna kvinna (Woman Woman).*

1957   *Natt i marknadstältet (Night in the Market Tent).* Awarded a house for life time use.

1958   *Gilla gång (Normal Course); Nattens ögonsten (The Jewel of the Night)* published in limited edition for the Book Club *Svalan.*

1960   Receives "De Nio" 's great award.

1961   *Bark och löv (Bark and Leaves).*

1962   Receives "Boklotteriets" great award.

1964   Receives a State artist's award of a guaranteed annual income for life.

1966   "Världen är en övergående historia" ("The World is a Transient Affair") a series of three radio lectures on ethics and aesthetics.

1968   Interviewed on Swedish Radio by Carl Magnus von Seth.

1969   Honorary Doctor of Philosophy at University of Umeå. "Möte med Lars Ahlin och hans texter" ("Meeting with Lars Ahlin and his texts"). Interview on Swedish Television produced by Tone Bengtsson.

1970   "In på benet" ("To the Bare Bones"), the first written information about Ahlin's mystical experience in 1933.

CHAPTER 1

Development of the Writer

I Childhood and adolescence

L ARS Ahlin was born in 1915 in Sundsvall, an industrial seaport town in northern Sweden, which has served as the setting for most of his novels.[1] He grew up in a society which was moving from a conservative, class-structured nation to a modern welfare state. Changes in the economy following World War I resulted in mass unemployment during the 1920s and 1930s, and Ahlin's family slipped down the social scale from middle class to working class status. In an attempt to improve their lot the family moved to Stockholm but returned to Sundsvall after four years. Eventually, the family moved to the working class district in the hilly outskirts of the town. The juxtaposition of such a social move downward and a geographical move upward is an ironic device later used by Ahlin in his novels *Egen spis (A Stove of One's Own*, 1948) and *Min död är min (My Death Is My Own*, 1945).

In addition to economic and political instability in society at large, Ahlin experienced an unstable family life: his mother left home when Ahlin was five years old and his father's second marriage was not always harmonious. In Stockholm the seven children were left to themselves for long periods and lived in a sort of sibling community. The father was charming but failed to provide a conventionally secure family environment. He seems to resemble the father figure in many of Ahlin's novels, particularly Peter in *Om (If, About, Around*, 1946), Sylvan in *Min död är min*, and the father in *Bark och löv (Bark and Leaves*, 1961). But it may be unwise to read this similarity too literally. Ahlin said in an interview in 1957 that, "My father is perhaps the person who has provided my best material. He was a great storyteller but I would never undertake to portray him; that would go beyond my powers of expression."[2]

15

Very few memories from Ahlin's childhood have been made
public. There are, in fact, only two: Once a neighbor family invited
the boy Lars to a midsummer feast. His memories of the event may
be reflected in the mirth and excitement of the children's celebra-
tion of midsummer in *Min död är min (My Death Is My Own)*. The
other is of a more somber character. As a ten year old, Ahlin
remembers how laughing strike breakers watched the funeral
procession for a worker who had been murdered during a garbage
strike in Sundsvall in 1925.[3] The scene illustrates the conflict
between individual dignity and institutional power or values. This
was to become one of the major themes in Ahlin's work.

At thirteen years of age, Ahlin had to leave school to contribute to
his own support. He sold newspapers, warming himself in the steam
outlet from the bath house, an incident which served as the basis for
a scene in *Om (If, About, Around)*. Like many other boys from
deprived homes, he peddled shoe laces, Christmas cards, and other
small items. After a short period as a member of the local YMCA and
IOGT (International Order of Good Templars), more tempted by
their libraries than seriously interested in their ideals, Ahlin joined a
Communist pioneer group where he found both books and com-
panionship.

His major interest, however, was literature rather than politics,
although he did become a Marxist and studied the required political
tracts. He also read Strindberg, Eyvind Johnson, Pär Lagerkvist, and
discovered the greatness of Dostoevski. The Communist group offered many cultural activities such as theater, poetry readings, and
discussions. His close friend, Ivar Öhman,[4] remembers that Ahlin
was less orthodox than Öhman himself, who insisted that literature
must be class conscious and revolutionary. Ahlin, on the other hand,
was more willing to accept and appreciate different kinds of literature.

In 1931, Ahlin temporarily became more involved with politics
when the last serious strike of pre-Social Democratic Sweden broke
out in Ådalen, not far from Sundsvall. This event, and the conflicts
within the Communist party, made him more politically active. During this period he served as an apprentice journalist for a Communist
newspaper, *Norrlands - Kuriren*, supported financially by Öhman's
father. After the elections in 1932, Öhman's father lost his seat in the
Swedish *Riksdag* and thereby the means to continue employing
Ahlin, who then contributed to the paper on a freelance basis. Ahlin
also wrote articles for a journal which the young Öhman edited.

However, like many others at this time, he was essentially unemployed. Other interests were soon to replace his political activism.

II *Leaving home*

By age eighteen Ahlin felt that he must leave his old life. In May,
1933 he borrowed a tent from Ivar Öhman, and went on the road.
He planned to get money by selling a poem (not his own) door to
door. This was a common means of support for many unemployed
young men at this time; it gave them at least a pretense of working
and not begging. In addition it provided them with a legitimate occupation, thus preventing them from being legally regarded as
vagrants, a criminal offense. Ahlin, parted from his political circle
and his friend, now led a less serene existence.[5] He was an intruder
upon people, invading their privacy to sell his poem. Like Tåbb, the
protagonist of his first published novel, he belonged nowhere and
was unwelcome everywhere.

III *Ahlin's mystical experience*

During this period, lying sick and feverish in his tent, he experienced a profound revelation of the essence of existence. In its
significance and impact on his future creative work, the revelation
resembles in intensity Luther's tower experience,[6] with which it also
shares the lack of a precise date. Ahlin described his experience for
the first time in explicit terms in a television interview of 1969, referring to it as "a block of visions or hallucinations."[7]

Erik Hjalmar Linder discusses the experience while it was still
only known from vague informal sources in *Ny Illustrerad Svensk
Litteraturhistoria* (1966). He labels it an intuitive understanding of a
unity between the disparate elements of existence, and perceives it
to have evoked in Ahlin a sense of paradoxical equality existing in a
world composed of extreme inequalities. The hallucinatory message
had revealed to Ahlin that the dignity of the superior people in the
world depends on their low esteem of inferiors, who themselves
share this view. Therefore, superiority and inferiority are interdependent and evaluation of the individual in those terms
becomes ultimately meaningless as does the question of equality.[8]

During the interview Ahlin read a text describing how the experience had changed his consciousness. He analyzed it in the following terms in a text printed a year later: "Now when I saw this
'city' which was no longer a city but a bundle of realities, independent from us, I realized fully that meaning is given by us human be-

ings and that we, not the material, are in essence shaped by these
meanings. . . . When we adjust the material we invent its pattern.
The values are ours; the truths are by us and for us."[9]

Ahlin has also described his vision as a historical form of mysticism, that is, a mysticism anticipating future society, historical
reality, as opposed to conventional, ontological mysticism. By the
image of a flower which blossoms in the fall instead of the coming
spring, he compares his type of mystical insight to a natural form of
prolepsis. The flower blooms in rebellion to time and reason. It
stands opposed to the environment and indicates that there will
come another form of existence, different from the present one,
which is dark and decaying like the fall season.[10]

In like manner Ahlin's vision was a mystical announcement of a
coming historical reality, not the elimination of the world in favor of
an extrahistorical utopian reality. In an earlier essay, Ahlin defined
such an historical reality in terms of a circularly structured society in
which no individual would be placed higher than another. Consequently, this type of society will have eliminated differences arising
from higher and lower rankings typical of hierarchial structures.[11]

IV *Years of study*

In August, 1933 Ahlin had earned enough money selling poems to
settle in Stockholm and rent a typewriter. Nobody was interested in
his work, however, and when his money was gone Ahlin acquired a
new supply of poems and went on the road again. This time he saved
money for school, and in November, 1933 he enrolled in Ålsta, a folk
high school[12] in northern Sweden. There he soon formed a close al-
liance with the young sculptor-to-be Arne Jones. This was to become
a lifelong friendship.

At the school he devoted himself to theology: Luther, Anders
Nygren's *Eros och Agape (Eros and Agape)*, St. Paul, Barth, and
Kierkegaard. He also studied philosophy and political ideas, and
reviewed Ortega y Gasset's *The Revolt of the Masses* for the school
yearbook of 1934. In the summer of 1934, Ahlin had to take to the
road again, this time accompanied by Jones, peddling a poem written by the two of them. In the poem they appealed to the potential
buyer to help the young men continue their studies. In 1935, after
finishing their two years at Ålsta, Ahlin and Jones set up a book
bindery which soon failed, and Ahlin spent the summer on the road,
as usual.

Around this time Ahlin was introduced to Christian ritual and symbolism by a deacon named Hedberg. His contact with religion contributed to another overwhelming experience. One morning Ahlin participated in a religious service conducted by Hedberg. The setting was transcendentally serene with candles, prayer in front of a crucifix, and the officiant in ceremonial red, white and black garments. The morning air was crisp and translucent, clean. That same night Ahlin slept in a flophouse among filthy and decrepit people, who spent their time drinking and telling dirty jokes. The contrast between the two worlds, in Ahlin's language often called the "high" and the "low," made him ask where genuine reality is to be found. Reality had become "too vast to embrace in one single concept."[13]

V *Moving to Stockholm*

In 1936 Ahlin and Jones moved to Stockholm to pursue their artistic careers. Temporarily free from financial worries, thanks to a loan from a sympathetic teacher couple, David Palm and his wife, they devoted all their energies to study and the pursuit of their artistic interests.. They frequently participated in the city's religious life, favoring communion services. This year Ahlin was nominated to become a novice in the Societas Sanctae Birgittae, an order with high-church sympathies, and in 1941 he was received as a member *(lekbroder)* of this order.[14] Ahlin seems to have translated this interest in the religious ritual into the ritualistic behavior of his characters. The resemblance between movements in liturgical ritual and a character's hand movements becomes particularly striking in *Kanelbiten (Cinnamon Girl, 1952).*

He became more and more involved in his search for a religious answer to the question of what determines man's identity and worth. He also became increasingly disappointed with all "isms" and their pretensions of possessing the solution to man's problems and despair. In 1937 he declared: "I detest every party and cannot be loyal to any group."[15] To this day he will not allow any labels, political or religious, to be placed on him or his philosophy. He is a Christian, but in the same sense as Kierkegaard was, rejecting any association with the established religious community.

Ahlin finished his first novel, *Lille Prometheus (Little Prometheus)* in 1936 but no publisher would accept it. He spent most of the following winters in Stockholm, studying in public libraries and taking odd jobs to earn a bare subsistence. In the summer he worked outside Stockholm as a farm hand, an artist's assistant, and a nurse's aid at a home for epileptics.[16] Sessions at Ålsta and Birkagården's folk high schools helped him to survive some winters, since these schools provided scholarships for room and board in addition to instruction. His second novel, *Underklassare av blodet (Of Working Class Blood)* was finished in 1939 but was not accepted by any publisher.

In 1941 he enrolled for a short time at the Fjellstedtska school in Uppsala, an institution designed primarily for preparing students for the ministry. He studied languages and read extensively. His teachers recognized his literary talent, even though his first novels had been rejected. But they also advised him to look for a more realistic and profitable occupation. Ahlin tolerated but could not follow this advice, as we understand from the following description, written about twenty years later, regarding his years of struggle:

Then followed a number of years characterized by madness, light and dark madness, arrogance, stubbornness, failure, sickness and misery, work, constant work on an impossible task. When I gave up and listened to advice from the wise ones it was only to gather strength to desert them and return to books that should not concern me. I walked around, met new people and saw new things, wrote on slips of paper, talked aloud to myself on the streets, unaware, until someone snubbed me and I understood, smiling happily, what was going on: I was creating, I wrote in the air around me.[17]

VI *Ahlin's fiction*

After a winter of writing in every available public building (he was not allowed to stay in his rented room between 9 A.M. and 10 P.M.), Ahlin finished *Tåbb med Manifestet (Tåbb with the Manifesto)* in the spring of 1943. This time he did not send his manuscript to a publisher but to the critic Holger Ahlenius,[18] whose book about the worker in Swedish literature had been reviewed by his friend Arne Jones at Älsta. The book was published the same year.

In his review Erik Lindegren, poet and critic, called *Tåbb med Manifestet* one of the most important contemporary contributions to Swedish letters. He realized that the novel, in spite of its surface plot about the unemployed Tåbb and his struggles for a better life, did not belong to the traditional proletarian novel of similar themes, which had played a large role in Swedish literature since the 1930s.[19] Most other critics, however, saw Tåbb more as a proletarian protagonist and less as the anti-hero of ideologies he was meant to be. Consequently they criticized Ahlin's failure to conform to conventional "realism," an ironic critique based on misunderstanding of the writer's intention *not* to conform to the ideal of the realistic novel.

In the novel Ahlin argues that man's dependence on ideals for his appreciation of self is degrading rather than uplifting. His message disrupts the narrative flow as he digresses from storytelling into philosophical discussions and comments, delivered by Tåbb or another character, or the narrator. Ahlin adopted this aesthetic detachment from character and events primarily from the French and German novel of the 1920s and Eyvind Johnson's autobiographical novels, with their inserted stories loosely connected to the main plot provided a Swedish model for the new aesthetics Ahlin wanted to develop in his own writing.

The critics' reservations regarding Ahlin's first novel changed into enthusiasm over his collection of short stories the following year: *Inga ögon väntar mig (No Eyes Await Me*, 1944). In the short stories, plots are more tightly knit, giving the reader a more comfortable sense of continuity. The short stories also revealed Ahlin's outstanding talent for drawing a psychological portrait in a few scenes or with few words. Here his style resembles the Hemingway behavioristic school of fiction which Ahlin had become aware of through Thorsten Jonsson's collection of short stories *Fly till vatten och morgon (Flee to Water and Morning)*[20] written in this tradition.

The next year Ahlin published a novel which probably aroused the greatest mixture of critical reaction of all his novels. *Min död är min (My Death Is My Own*, 1945) is about the cuckold salesman Sylvan, his attempt to escape his sense of failure through suicide, and his final love for the pathetically unattractive Engla. With its many grotesque characters and bizarre episodes, it is "a comedy of the flesh strangely combined with the struggle of the soul," says the writer and critic Artur Lundkvist, who compared Ahlin to Dostoevski and Faulkner in his interest for "the lost man."[21] Erik Lindegren points to the similarity between Sylvan's life and Sartre's thesis that man can be himself only "in the moment of anxiety and humiliation."[22]

Other critics, however, were disturbed with what they perceived to be an improper preoccupation with man's less civilized nature. "Ahlin wants to combine objective characterization with theological speculation about man's nature . . . obviously related to . . . a sort of dark satisfaction at the discovery that man is a creep, a snake pit of

dirty thoughts and slimy desires," stated Stig Ahlgren.[23] The
Catholic critic Sven Stolpe failed to understand the artistic purpose
of Ahlin's characters, particularly a hunchback in whom he saw "a
new version of the perverse, life-negating sadistic type who is standard in the modern 'tough' American novel."[24] It is quite curious to
realize that at the end of World War II, with all its atrocities, critics
believed that literature, even the "realistic novel," should present a
more uplifting image of man than the one provided by reality.

The review which demonstrated the most perceptive reading of
the novel was Margit Abenius' in *Bonniers Litterära Magasin*, which
had been very encouraging to the writer at the time.[25] She perceived
the novel as a discussion of the problem of individual dignity versus
ideals and conventions which degrade him by underscoring his inferiority.

Failure of conventions to operate meaningfully in an individual's
life is also the issue in *Om* (*If, About, Around*, 1946) dealing with the
adolescent Bengt and his charmingly irresponsible father Peter.
Bengt tries to reform Peter so that he will become a more fitting
father image for Bengt to identify with. Stylistically this novel is
Ahlin's most interesting work. With an almost exuberant rejection of
narrative continuity, Ahlin changes point of view, plays with words
and grammar, and digresses into bizarre stories and philosophical
monologues. But it did not become the success he had hoped for.
Not until art critic Ulf Linde's essay "Det Ahlinska alternativet"
("The Ahlinian Alternative") in 1960,[26] now a classic in Ahlinian
criticism, do we get an insightful discussion about the aesthetics of
Om.

Again failing to receive critical acclaim for his attempt to break
away from traditional realism, Ahlin followed *Om* with two more
conventionally conceived novels, *Jungfrun i det gröna* (*Nigella
Damascena*, 1947) — about a folk high school principal's failure to
leave his pedestrian life to become a writer — and *Egen spis* (*A
Stove of One's Own*, 1948) — a comedy about a frivolous family on
welfare and their successful challenge of regulations and authorities.
He also published two collections of short stories, *Fångnas glädje*
(*Joy of the Imprisoned*, 1947), and *Huset har ingen filial* (*The House
Has No Annex*, 1949).

Egen spis (*A Stove of One's Own*) was turned into a filmscript but
never filmed.[27] In addition he wrote drama: *Lekpaus* (*Break in the
Game*, 1948) which was performed at The Royal Dramatic Theater,
and a radio play *Eld av eld* (*Fire from Fire*, 1949) published in a collection of the best radio plays of the year.

Lekpaus takes place in a home for older women. It is about an aging woman who does not want to accept her loss of youth, and therefore rejects her daughter, the reminder of her old age. In *Eld av eld*, a widow struggles to reconcile herself with the death of her husband and realizes that their love has created a sanctuary within her where they will always reach each other. This realization makes her reject a suitor she was inclined to favor out of loneliness.

Ahlin also wrote a play that was never performed, *Varje ängel är förfärlig (Every Angel Is Terrible)*, named after a quote from Rilke. Here he deals with an artist's search for a more genuine life through rebirth which he thinks he will find in women's motherly love. But when he meets his real mother, who is a decrepit old woman far from any ideal image of motherhood or womanly love, he turns instead to religion where he finally finds harmony.[28]

After this period of great creative output, during which he also married and begot a son, there is a pause of three years before Ahlin's next novel *Fromma mord (Pious Murders*, 1952) about Aron who returns from an asylum to his home town with two purposes: to put a stone on his father's tomb and marry Evangeline, neither of which he accomplishes. Instead, he becomes involved in bizarre events with his old friends who, at the end, laughingly leave him while he sinks into a swamp. *Fromma mord (Pious Murders)* is Ahlin's most "difficult" novel, and is regarded by some critics and himself as his most important work. Although it may be read as a play on "languages," that is, interactions between social and philosophical attitudes, rather than a novel with characters interacting as people, it also lends itself to a more conventional discussion of theme. Erik Hjalmar Linder compares the novel to *Ulysses* or *Finnegan's Wake* "but with a religious-theological key and written in a language which does not reject standard grammar."[29]

After *Fromma mord (Pious Murders)* came one of Ahlin's more easily accessible novels, *Kanelbiten (Cinnamon Girl*, 1953). The simplicity of the epic surface structure corresponds to an intriguing tale about the death of innocence, about a young girl's contacts with adulthood and love, and about her despair borne by the irrationality of life. The following year *Stora glömskan (The Great Amnesia*, 1954) was published, another novel with an adolescent protagonist, the boy Zackarias. Unlike Britt-Marie in *Kanelbiten* he accepts the irrational elements of existence, though it brings him suffering and despair. Ultimately he learns that both joy and tears are essential in life.

"Lars Ahlin Is Getting Closer" is the title of Örjan Lindberger's

review of these two novels[30] which expressed the general consensus
that here Ahlin had successfully blended message and form. In the
novels, he retains his usual flair for the unreal and bizarre in character and events, but confines the narrative to a more conventional
though episodic structure.

There is a dreamlike mood in *Stora glömskan* and, this mood is intensified in *Kvinna kvinna* (*Woman Woman*, 1955) a tale with
archetypal elements. In it Torgny Larsson, a construction worker,
struggles with temptations and obstacles of mythical nature when he
travels from the coast to join his wife in the woods.

Two years later followed Ahlin's great epic about love, *Natt i
marknadstältet* (*Night in the Market Tent*, 1957), finished on little
slips of paper (while his wife was packing) during his move into a
house donated as a writer's home for lifetime use.[31] Two main
characters stand out among the throng of people in the novel:
Paulina, who with unconditional love for life accepts the joys and
sorrows of the human condition, and Zackarias, who learns about the
joys and sorrows of love which will help him serve man in the future
as a writer. After this novel about love in macrocosm, we get *Gilla
gång* (*Normal Course*, 1958) about the school janitors Lage and
Berta. Their story presents love in microcosm, on a more personal
level than given in *Natt i marknadstältet*, with its sweeping
philosophical-theological exploration of love.

In Ahlin's last novel, *Bark och löv* (*Bark and Leaves*, 1961), the
artist Aino believes that commitment to personal love will destroy her
as an artist. But her reservations about such a commitment are ironic
in that she is already unproductive. Her lover, Erik, a writer, does
believe in personal love as a productive component in an artist's life,
though he too is unproductive. In this novel, Ahlin is, however, less
interested in presenting these characters as psychological portraits
than in having them illustrate attitudes toward love, art, and society,
which involve man in a series of relationships which he must learn to
make creative lest they destroy him. Structurally, the novel is
another example of Ahlin's never-ceasing attempt to find new forms
for his art. The present is built upon an intriguing arrangement of
cubicles of events in the past, tied together by language and word associations rather than rational continuity of plot.

VII   *Ahlin's theories on fiction*

Lars Ahlin's interest in the form of the novel was demonstrated
early in his career. He sent one of his manuscripts to a publisher in
1939 with a letter in which he divulged his objectives as a writer,

saying that he wanted to function as an "intercessor," that is, as an intermediator between lowly and superior worlds.[32] His view of the writer as intercessor is further advanced in "Om ordkonstens kris" ("About the Crisis of the Art of Words"), one of three important essays he published in the mid-1940s.[33] In this essay he also coined the word "identifier" *(identificator)* to describe his aesthetic position. This word has come to be the most commonly used one to describe his attitude.

With these concepts Ahlin defines a detached narrative attitude which is nevertheless involved with the spiritual condition of the poor, the miserable, and the unsuccessful. Through detachment he appeals to the reader's intellectual response rather than emotional, and his characters do not become individuals in a socio-realistic sense.[34] Consequently their speech is not consistent with their level of education or social status either in terms of semantics or sophistication of thought. Most of his characters speak a confusingly similar language which makes them resemble not only each other but also the writer-narrator.

This makes his characters unrealistic, though not unbelievable, and helps to create an emotional detachment between reader and character. This aesthetic detachment is important to maintain, Ahlin believes, because the artist is only a "second maker,"[35] confined to create in words; thus his characters should be perceived as word constructs rather than imitations of "real" persons.

Ahlin's formalistic detachment from his characters is consistent with his belief that the realism of the traditional novel, with its roots in the nineteenth century, is no longer a viable artistic attitude. He wishes to replace it with another form of realism which he calls, in several letters during the 1930s, "Christian realism," which he finds exemplified in the writings of Dostoevski and Sigrid Undset.[36] With this term Ahlin seems to be advancing a concept we shall later find developed in Auerbach's *Mimesis* (1946), where it is applied to the Russian writers of the late nineteenth century.

Christian realism, Auerbach argues, is characterized by a mingling of styles and a preference for characters of low social status. Its objective is to illustrate "God's incarnation in a human being of the humblest social station,"[37] and consequently to convey the idea that man possesses inherent dignity regardless of social rank. There is, in this kind of writing, a taste for the grotesque, a mixture of man's highest spiritual qualities with his lowest, most instinctual desires of the flesh.

As opposed to the Flaubertian style of realistic novel in which man is presented as a consistent creature within a rather conventional, psychological framework, Christian realism seizes upon the paradox of human qualities which are both "high" and "low," consisting of extremes confined within one body. Another way of looking upon this combination of contradictory elements in man would be with humor, Luther's way of incorporating man's extreme qualities into a meaningful whole.

Ahlin's relationships both to Christian realism and "humorous realism" are presented with great insight in Hans-Göran Ekman's *Humor, pikaresk och grotesk*.[38] He demonstrates how Ahlin has been inspired by, among others, Nathan Söderblom's Luther studies, Thomas Mann, and Kierkegaard.

With the vehemence of a missionary eager to convert people to a new faith, Ahlin rejects the notion that the novel should be a projection of social reality. In this respect he stands among the first to formulate a change in artistic consciousness among Swedish writers. Ahlin is "disgusted" by the "mechanism of illusions" of the established traditional novel,[39] meaning the illusion of authentic social existence which supposedly is reproduced in this type of novel. His strong reaction is explained by the fact that he regards such an artistic ideal as a deception of the reader and thus an immoral endeavor.[40]

One way to avoid throwing the spell of illusion over the reader is to constantly remind him that he is reading words, not interacting with people. Apart from his method of characterization, Ahlin accomplishes this objective by fragmentation of narrative continuity, which forces the reader to a more active reading. Ideally, Ahlin thinks, there should be a "dialogue" between writer and reader in the sense that the reader should respond intellectually to the novel, not become involved in any suspension of disbelief, or to borrow Valery's words often quoted by Ahlin, not to undergo a "crisis of credulity" *(lättrogenhetens kris)*.[41]

The form of "dialogue" Ahlin has in mind here seems analogous to the Lutheran notion that man's work is his answer to God's word. Similarly, Ahlin sees himself as a writer speaking to each reader who answers by reacting actively, intellectually working with the text.

This means that the reader of Ahlin's novels is asked to provide his own "why-because"[42] explanation of characters' actions and reasons for the events. In the realistic novel of illusion, this synthesis is provided by the writer, who thereby guides the reader to a meaningful reading along the writer's path. By doing so, however, the writer forces the reader to accept the text on conditions other than those of the reader. Ahlin prefers that the reader derive a meaning from his own "locus" (ort), that is, on the basis of his own experiences and understanding, which means that there may be many "answers" to a novel without any of them the absolute, the only answer. For example, he says in Om (If, About, Around): "It is my words' pulsation in your system of associations that is my model, my working material, my intention. . . . Not about Bengt not about Peter not about Herkula or any other person is this book but about you" (330).

VIII   Initial aesthetic inspiration

Ahlin's first encounter with writings which challenged the existence of absolute values and their foundation was made in connection with his leaving his hometown at the age of eighteen. He then read Poincaré's Science and Hypothesis,[43] and much of Poincaré's treatise points toward the kind of questions that will later occupy Ahlin in his search for a new form for the novel. Poincaré says, for example, that the framework into which we fit facts are adjusted to our construction and based on our measurements. This means that facts are adjusted to our constructs which then obscure their essential qualities. Similarly Ahlin conceives equality to be a function of man's essential qualities which often, however, are disguised by facts which are socially perceived and measurable qualities. Ahlin's "identifier" principle operates to eliminate the social facts from his characters' essential qualities, and so change the reader's conception of people conventionally regarded as socially inferior, making him perceive the equality inherent in all men.

Furthermore, Poincaré points at man's lack of an objective language and therefore his inability to observe the world objectively. This is also an issue for linguistic philosophy which Ahlin later came in contact with, particularly through the writings of Wittgenstein. Wittgenstein's declaration in Tractatus that "The limit of my language is the limit of my world" explains why Ahlin's identifier-intercessor fails to conform to his characters' "realistic" level of speech. Through these principles Ahlin wants to expand our understanding of the "low" and their failures by giving them a "higher" language and thus a higher form of consciousness and social status.

The reading of André Gide's The Counterfeiters became yet another major influence on Ahlin during this period. In this novel Gide exposes the hypocrisy of moral-ethical values in the counterfeit

morals of the bourgeois. Homosexual love is romanticized, while
heterosexual love is commercialized in marriage and decadent
loveless sex. Jaded children play deadly games and find excitement
in crime, while their parents appear ridiculous in believing that their
knowledge of life is superior and more sophisticated than that of
their children. Such reversal of values and conventions is a dominant
feature of Ahlin's novels.

The Counterfeiters also features an unconventional structural
device in the function of Édouard. He is at times narrator in the first
person, a morally detached observer of the other characters, and at
other times a character in a third-person narration. In addition to his
narrative functions, Édouard discusses the writing of a novel called
The Counterfeiters and the aesthetics of the novel in general. Ahlin
will later use similar approaches to writing a novel particularly in
Om (If, About, Around) and *Bark och löv (Bark and Leaves)*.

Ahlin also credits his readings of Dostoevski and Thomas Mann
with having helped him formulate his aesthetics, but he does not
elaborate on the exact nature of their influence. Arne Melberg
provides in his *På väg från realismen (Moving away from Realism)*[44]
a more detailed discussion of what aspects of these two writers Ahlin
seems to have incorporated in his work and theories.

Dostoevski's most important contribution to an antirealistic tradition, Melberg argues, seems to be his power to translate ideas into
characters who interact on two levels: as people and as representatives of ideas. We also find this form of characterization,
"animated arguments" *(gestaltade argument)*,[45] in Ahlin's novels,
particularly in *Fromma mord (Pious Murders)* and *Bark och löv
(Bark and Leaves)*.

Ahlin apparently derives his interest in irony as an aesthetic principle from Thomas Mann. The narrator in Ahlin's first published
short story "Hemliga manipulationer" ("Secret Manipulations")[46]
refers to Mann's lecture on Freud and then suggests that an "ironic-
artistic" attitude toward failure would enable man to accept himself
as failure without being forced to manipulate with his consciousness
and escape into comforting utopias about an existence without
failure. Technically, the irony in Mann becomes a function of the
narrator, who is part of the narrative but detached from and commenting on its events. He is similar to the narrator of romantic irony,
a genre which Ahlin also credits with viable narrative attitude,
together with Kierkegaard's technique of using pseudonyms.[47]

Mann's adaptation of the "montage" technique[48] enables him to incorporate written passages in his work, to use different "languages," that is, styles, and to apply a continuity through association instead of rational organization of time and space sequences. This technique of "mounting" together apparently disjointed passages, a prominent feature also of cinematic narrative technique, we recognize in many of Ahlin's novels, notably his experimental *Om (If, About, Around), Fromma mord (Pious Murders),* and *Bark och löv (Bark and Leaves).* But also a novel with conventional structure like *Stora glömskan (The Great Amnesia)* reveals on closer examination an affinity with cinematic narrative convention. It may be added that Ahlin was trying his hand at writing scripts and scenarios for the film in the 1940s[49] and was friendly with Ingmar Bergman during this period.[50] These experiences may well have inspired him, independently of the influence Mann's novels may have exerted, to employ cinematic features in his novels.

It is evident that Ahlin pondered questions of the novel's forms and objectives early in his career, though it took twelve years before he published his own theories in the 1940s. We find these theories perpetuated and developed further in his next period of substantial essayistic production which began in 1961 with an important speech at a writer's conference at Biskops-Arnö. They were further advanced in some articles[51] and a series of radio lectures in 1966.[52] In addition, his ideas on the novel are woven into the novels themselves, particularly *Om (If, About, Around), Fromma mord (Pious Murders)* and *Bark och löv (Bark and Leaves),* and Ahlin remains one of the few great theorists of fiction in Swedish literature.

CHAPTER 2

Tåbb with the Manifesto

I   *The plot: The process of liberation from ideals*

IN *Tåbb med Manifestet* (*Tåbb with the Manifesto*, 1943)[1] Ahlin describes an individual's struggle to bridge the gap between his ideals and reality. He exposes the conventions and principles which form his protagonist's psychological frame of reference and in whose terms, or "language," he defines his own self.

Tåbb's language is that of the *Communist Manifesto* which defines his ideal concept of self as that of a proletarian worker. But since Tåbb is unemployed he does not belong to this category and instead feels doomed to become a *Lumpenproletarian*,[2] a traitor to the socialist cause. This is, the *Manifesto* teaches, the inescapable result of unemployment, because want of basic needs makes the unemployed an easy prey for any powers which can offer him food and shelter. Tåbb's "language" has no words for his own in-between situation and therefore he exists only in terms provided by the *Manifesto*, which labels him in negative terms, contrary to his positive ideal: lumpenproletarian versus proletarian.

Tåbb has spent four months on the road looking for work when we first meet him, standing alone in the midst of the boisterous activities of a country fair. Nobody recognizes him, and his need for an identity is so strong that he is willing to spend his last money on a date only to make her whisper: "Tåbb. You are Tåbb with the *Manifesto*" (14); but finds no one.

His distress is illustrated in the dichotomy between his intellectually abstract attitude to life and the physically noxious character of his environment. His silence, set against the noise of the people at the fair, underscores his feeling of standing apart from the rest of the world. He is classless in a class-structured society, unemployed among workers. Intellectually, he accepts the *Manifesto's* words that he is victimized by natural forces inherent in the economic system and not by individuals in the system. Emotionally, however, he cannot help feeling hostile toward the happy workers around him.

Only two people notice Tåbb: a disgustingly filthy, drunken man and a ridiculously dressed woman shamelessly casting inviting glances at him. "Something of Lagerkvist's dark hatred of the animal in man," said Erik Lindegren in his review, "lurks in Ahlin's description of the people at the fair."[3] Unable to find peace, Tåbb leaves the crude clowns, the crippled harmonica player, the decrepit whore, and the gaudy crowd, and spends his last money on drink.

The beer in his empty stomach works rapidly, and as he becomes more and more intoxicated the phrase, "you are alive only when you have a job," (25) pounds in his head. He is dead; dead as a worker. Worthless. His own helplessness seems illustrated by a blind man, abandoned and crying for assistance. When the blind man leaves, the waitress discovers that he has wet his chair and shrieks in disgust, adding to the general chaos and noise. Feeling that he must raise his fellowman to a higher level of consciousness, Tåbb stands up to deliver a speech. At that moment, however, the alcohol finally hits him and he falls to the floor, bringing the chaos to a climax. Completely devoid of dignity, he staggers out and vomits with his arms around a tree. The scene is typical of Ahlin in its juxtaposition of intellectual ideal and the vulgar manifestations of man's physical nature.

Back in his tent, Tåbb is tempted to ask for what he calls a "Savior," someone who will ease the pain of living, remove his despair, and give him hope and mental comfort. But soon he regains his mental strength and thinks with joy that as long as he suffers, he will be safe from sinking too low ideologically. Like Kierkegaard's religious man, he believes that his suffering will be uplifting[4] and keep his proletarian consciousness alive to remind him that only proletarian work can truly save him. Happy to have found a rational stand for himself, he drifts off to sleep.

Tåbb will, however, again be tempted to escape from his distress. Alcohol provided the escape in the first chapter. Now he meets another temptation: sex, the language of physical life-force spoken by Anna and his own body. This language speaks of natural satisfaction, bliss through procreation as opposed to the intellectually articulated futurism of Tåbb's language in the first chapter.

When Tåbb knocks at Anna's door peddling a poem he is filled with despair. His dread "sloshed through blood and nerves like sickening rats" (55). Anna too is in despair but of a different kind. She is possessed by an almost overpowering urge for erotic fulfillment, and this makes her, paradoxically, passive, ashamed, and afraid of men. She dreams about a man who will be her equal in shame and with whom she will conceive a child. Then she will return to her home in the forest pregnant with a boy, and there restore vitality to a pre-industrial form of life, now a dying form of society.

She senses Tåbb's shame at being forced to this disguised begging and realizes that he is the man she has been waiting for: "She thought of him as a force, a condition she wanted to experience. Then he would leave her. She would forget his face, but never his force" (77).

Tåbb also dreams about a future with her. But he sees the future as a comfortably structured life, not as one in fulfillment of nature's callings: he sees in Anna his woman, his comrade, who would keep their home impeccably neat and become involved in local politics, edit his motions for union meetings, and help him write letters to the editor. His physical desires and his own body are basically alien to him,[5] and therefore he translates Anna's erotic appeal and his own erotic stimulation into political images before he gives in to them. Fumbling and tenderly Tåbb and Anna lose their virginity in each others' arms. Fed and physically satisfied, Tåbb believes once again that he will become one of the young pioneers working for the rise of a socialist state.

Tåbb, however, soon understands that Anna is not of proletarian stock. She belongs to the earth, not to the city and the factory. Her intensely physical nature and her attraction to the woods frighten him. Therefore he leaves her, rejecting her offer to settle on her father's farm.

In the following chapters Tåbb moves toward a compromise with his ideal. Nielsen points out that "Tåbb acquires a new language which does not contain any new words for the coming socialist ideal state but instead speaks about man's personal sufferings and inadequacy."[6] His third temptation to escape leads to a compromise with his ideals. He meets Ivar, who offers him the winter in his mountain cottage full of books in exchange for Tåbb's help with a burglary.

Ivar serves as a foil to Tåbb. Unlike Tåbb, Ivar has become a lumpenproletarian who, lacking social consciousness, grabs what he can get from society regardless of whether he hurts a bourgeois shopkeeper or one of his former working comrades. Tåbb agrees to help him, but only after Ivar has promised to stay away from the worker-owned co-op and to break into a hardware store instead. This means that Tåbb is able to remain loyal to the proletariat in spite of his situation. Contrary to the theories of the *Communist Manifesto*, he does not degrade himself by becoming a lumpenproletarian to satisfy his immediate physical needs.

Tåbb and Ivar spend the evening before the burglary in a flophouse full of tramps in various stages of decay, physical and moral. The noise, the characters, and the stench, as obtrusive here as in the earlier market scene, seem to reflect Tåbb's inner state of mind, his confusion and despair. Waiting for the time to leave, Tåbb drifts off into his usual analysis of his situation.

His ideal, his "image of health" (135) does not condone burglary as a solution to his hardships, even though his lack of money is no fault of his own. If he violates his image of health he will, he believes, come dangerously close to turning into a morally rotten social outcast, a lumpenproletarian. "I don't want the proletarian worker inside me to die," Tåbb thinks (138). But since only a socialist society and socialist economy can produce a socialist man, Tåbb knows that he, a product of bourgeois society, can never become a true proletarian. He realizes that he and his contemporaries are still infested by bourgeois ideas: "in our emotional life, our character, our emotional and cultural consciousness . . . we must endure bourgeois inhibitions and capitalistically contaminated instincts" (141). This does not, however, exclude loyalty to the socialist cause, Tåbb concludes; this realization indicates a first move toward a compromise between his ideal and his present reality. He is beginning to prepare himself for the fact that he must live a less-than-ideal life or not live at all.

When Tåbb realizes that Ivar intends to violate their agreement and burglarize the co-op, he strikes him in fury. Ivar loses all his will power in Tåbb's hands and turns into an evil smelling hulk. His bad breath symbolizes his rotten morality just as the flophouse stench earlier in the novel was connected to people with a degenerate social consciousness. Tåbb leaves Ivar after securing enough money for a ticket to another town.

Tåbb is now prepared to begin his search for a language of compromise. His first inspiration comes when he participates in the May Day demonstrations. He marches under the banner of a socialist club singing the *Internationale*. With great disappointment Tåbb finds himself unable to respond emotionally to the song and the group spirit. His intellectual-analytical mind interferes with his emotional expectations: "Why must we always walk toward a paradise" (151); "To a person without a paradise everyone is equally good and all conditions equally attractive . . . but as soon as you have a goal or a paradise you have divided mankind and existence into two groups, for or against" (152); "he ought to cry out: How shall we live in dignity with the truth that we are never going to enter paradise. . . . Look at us. . . . Sing for us. . . . Sing for the doomed ones" (155). Tåbb, realizing that his lack of proper proletarian qualities is existentially unavoidable, tries to liberate himself from his psychological dependence on something unattainable as a basis for his sense of personal value. He wants to give the doomed ones like himself the same privilege as the favored ones enjoy: a song, something which will make them feel equal.

In his thoughts during the May Day demonstrations, Tåbb articulates the attitude toward society and culture which Ahlin describes in all of his novels: how ideals tend to destroy our individual dignity by setting us up against a model beyond our reach and ranking us as inherently inferior. Man is eternally condemned to live outside paradise; therefore he must adjust his life accordingly, instead of clinging to false premises. Tåbb is, however, not ready to live according to his insights under the banner. He joins a traveling salesman and steals his wallet. He gives an unemployed youngster enough money to attend a folk high school during the winter, and then resumes his wanderings until he meets a painter who offers him a job as a model.

One evening Tåbb and the painter, Staffan Hyrell, discuss Tåbb's Marxist philosophy. His belief in society's progress toward an ideal socialist state is dismissed by Staffan as metaphysical speculation. But he asks if Tåbb can look upon his miserable situation in such a way that it appears better. At that question Tåbb's consciousness changes. He realizes that he has two identities, one social and one personal, and he feels reborn when he finds that his distress emanates from a misunderstanding. The *Manifesto*, he now understands, is only concerned with people in their social roles, not with them as individuals. In death, Tåbb speculates, he will be totally free from social evaluations because when he dies only a person dies, while the proletarian cause will continue to live. And, since death is not sociopolitically evaluated, he will in death be free from values and subsequent feelings of degradation and inferiority.

Set upon dying, Tåbb goes to Stockholm where he meets Kajsa from his home village. She too has her scars: her first lover fell to his death at a construction site before her eyes. Tåbb moves in with Kajsa and having decided to die when the money he stole from the salesman is gone, he permits himself to indulge in physical and emotional comfort. This is a more tangible state of bliss than the paradise presented by the *Manifesto*, which has now lost its glory and attraction. He does not believe in dogmas about future happiness in an ideal state any more. But his "language" remains Marxist: when the time comes for him to die, he pretends to Kajsa that he got his money by being a strikebreaker, thus making himself in the eyes of a revolutionary socialist more despicable than he would have been if he had told the truth. She leaves him in disgust.

But Tåbb does not die. Instead, he is drafted and, failing to appear at his regiment, he is picked up by the police in a state half dead from starvation and depression. He is brought to a hospital and, as Tåbb ironically comments, society is now ready to help him, although it could not maintain his health earlier by providing a job for him. Now, as a draftee, he fits into the system again; unemployed he did not belong to the system.

Two years later Tåbb and Kajsa meet again back in their home village. Kajsa too has lived through a form of death: a degrading marriage and an abortion. Tåbb is working, and in his spare time, hunting, fishing, and tending a garden. In many ways his life now resembles the life he rejected when it was offered him by Anna. Kajsa, who still loves Tåbb, meets him in a wood shed and asks why her apple tree does not bear fruit. Because it gets no pollen from another tree, Tåbb explains, and Kajsa, articulating the implied author's remarks,

understood Tåbb's criticism of the patriarchal-capitalistic society. Was it not a kind of abnormal male fruit? No wonder its civilization has become so mechanical, technical, and militaristic . . . A human being is created by man and woman. Shouldn't the creation of a culture so dominated by male sex characteristics be replaced by a more human culture in which male and female qualities had become inseparably united? (254)

Happy at the prospect of sharing future goals and filled with joy at her renewed meeting with Tåbb, Kajsa lifts her basket of wood which they carry into her house together. Ahlin will use the motif of a man and a woman united by wood in later novels to symbolize balance and equality.[7]

II *The problem of identity*

The "language" of an Ahlinian character, Kai Henmark observes in *En fågel av eld* (*A Bird of Fire*, 1962), defines his worth in terms of a narrowly conceived system of values, while omitting values belonging to other systems, other "languages." An individual who cannot identify with the values of his chosen "language" therefore feels degraded and worthless, even though he may possess qualities that would be highly regarded in another "language." A person who feels worthless for this reason, Henmark argues, will be tempted to change his language in favor of one which can "save" him from this feeling. This is, however, no solution to his conflict but only an escape from the painful dichotomy between his true situation and his ideal.[8]

Ahlin calls this escape "salvation," which is a mechanism allowing the individual to forget his actual situation and through psychological comfort disregard the ideals which make him suffer because they are beyond his reach. In *Tåbb with the Manifesto*, such means of escape are said to be provided by "houses of substitution: the chapels and churches, dance halls and movie theaters, bars and pubs" (42). Ahlin disapproves of escapes into such "houses" because they shield man from life's inherent conflicts and pains. If man forgets the conflicting qualities of existence he will not come of age as a human being, but instead live with a numbed consciousness.

A person's ideal image of self is often role-defined in social terms: Tåbb's ideal role is that of a proletarian worker and he does not want to project any other image.[9] Ahlin does not think that the individual's appreciation of self should be contingent upon his role identification. Nor does he believe, in fact, that man can find any ideal form of existence. Unlike the preceding generation's optimistic search for a solution to mankind's problems, either through "the transformation of existing conditions by means of an enlightened Marxist social and economic program,"[10] or in Lawrencian sexual mysticism and Freudian psychoanalysis, Ahlin and his generation want to accept life intellectually *with* its conflicts and despair. They want to *describe* conflicts, not solve them.[11] Therefore, when Tåbb, after much hardship, finds it impossible to become a proletarian worker, he compromises and chooses another role without pretending that his new role is a new ideal. In other words, he embraces his new identity without condemning and repressing his earlier ideal.[12] By accepting the complex diversities of existence and adjusting his own life accordingly, Tåbb has created a balance between conflicting elements without eliminating either of them.

In Tåbb we see the disillusionment typical of fictional characters in the literature of the 1940s. World War II was then teaching man that he had no power over his destiny. Tåbb learns that individual merit does not guarantee individual happiness, or, in his Marxist terms, he believes that his misery is no fault of his or any other human being, but a function of impersonal powers within the social and economic system. By not being able to influence, personally, the course of events determining the quality of his life, he becomes existentially alienated from society. His existence seems increasingly nonsensical and laden with irony.

Existential man cannot rely upon established conventions of good and evil to guide his choice of actions; yet, in order to exist, he must choose. Erik Lindegren's collection of poems, *Mannen utan väg* (*The Man without a Way*) published in 1942,[13] the year before *Tåbb with the Manifesto*, bears a title emblematic of the disorientation of the new generation of Swedish and European writers. Sharing their general sense of existing in an irrational world, Ahlin, however, does not share their nihilism. He resembles Kierkegaard in his belief that Christianity offers viable spiritual guidance even in a chaotic world. Faith may not make the world less absurd, but it will make its absurdity more acceptable, just as faith reconciles man's demand for a rational world with his belief in the irrationality of God becoming man in Christ. In *Tåbb with the Manifesto*, as in the six subsequent novels, we follow the protagonist's road through despair and suffering to his ultimate attainment of some form of reconciliation between his self and his existence.

The theme of *Tåbb with the Manifesto* is expressed in its dialectical structure, Arne Melberg argues in *På väg från realismen* (*Moving away from Realism*, 1973).[14] By this he means that the novel, like all of Ahlin's novels, contains a "dialectical deep structure" consisting of "confession, rejection, death and, eventually rebirth."[15] "Confession" refers to the ideal the protagonist uses initially to define and evaluate his existence, his first "language." "Rejected" by his ideal as formulated by his confession, the protagonist first feels worthless. He then reaches a turning point and gains a more acceptable view of self. This he accomplishes through a symbolic form of death. In Tåbb's case death is followed by "rebirth" in the form of a synthesis between "the actual conditions of existence and society's

demands and assumptions."[16] Tåbb moves back to his rural home,
accepting what work there is and living in harmony with nature,
whereas earlier he could only conceive of a life regulated by a factory whistle.

III *Irony*

Tåbb fights his impulse to give in to fear and despair through
irony, a form of detachment, a method of controlling his emotional
reactions. Ahlin describes his detachment in images of cold, as opposed to the flaming and violent character of Tåbb's feelings: "His
cold detachment implies a kind of petrification, as if he in his irony
turns away from life itself."[17] At the country fair, for example, anger
surges painfully within Tåbb as he stands surrounded by people enjoying themselves, completely indifferent to his situation: "But fear
of that which was flaming inside him calmed him. He soon realized
his feelings were unreasonable. His pain froze to irony and again his
knowledge gained the power to influence him" (18), but still he temporarily loses control of himself and is reduced to a vomiting bum,
"just body, an animal without consciousness, merely a sensitivity of
twisting nerves and instincts" (40).

At times he "feared the transparent world of consciousness. He
wanted to rest apathetically in the dark" (41). His intellect, however,
does not permit him to rest peacefully, oblivious of the world; instead, he seeks a way to preserve his dignity and Marxist identity
despite the fact that he is, from a Marxist point of view, drifting
toward a point where he cannot avoid becoming a traitor to the
socialist cause. Then, with a daring juxtaposition of reason and faith,
he proves to himself that he can still apply the logic of Marxism to
his thinking: he argues that Christ is a strikebreaker because He offers relief and salvation to all rejected people. Thus he manages to
overcome his temptation to seek comfort and peace of mind in Him
as a Savior. At this point he feels a sense of "wild joy," equal in intensity to his recent despair because he has channeled his emotions
into an intellectually acceptable context.

Tåbb's logic is, from the reader's perspective, full of irony.
Regarding emotions with suspicion, Tåbb does not realize that he
relates emotionally to the rational-logical system outlined in the
Manifesto. Then, by translating Christ's message of emotional and
spiritual comfort into sociopolitical terms, he creates a synthesis of
reason and passion which is unique in its conception, if not in-

comprehensible. The synthesis enables him to endure his current materialistic hardship and thus gives him peace of mind, a state of being he finds appalling in people who obtain this comfort outside a political frame of reference. He does not realize, as the reader of course does, that his political ideology serves as religious dogma.

Having overcome the temptation to seek comfort in religion, Tåbb meets Anna, who poses another threat to his ironical-analytical attitude toward life. When Anna offers him food and shelter, Tåbb will not accept it at first, because he does not want to become emotionally involved while he is still deprived of a social identity. She represents individualism as opposed to his collectivism, and Tåbb fears she will tempt him to cease striving for a reunion with the proletarian working class.

The question of whether or not he should accept her offerings thus becomes a matter of political rather than sexual morality: "I do not want any substitute for work. Making another human being a substitute would be a most shameful thing to do. . . . The woman shall be my working comrade. We shall not only live together physically, but in total togetherness, socially active as well" (83). He sees the two of them simultaneously as individuals with "no relation," that is, with unique identities, socially independent, and as members of a future socialist society. However tenderly he makes love to her, his intellectualization of the situation, as if he needed Marxist approval for his sex life, gives an ironic if not comic touch to the scene. Tåbb's dream of finding a synthesis between materialism and individualism in Anna's arms makes him more like a romantic idealist than the rational socialist he thinks he is.

It is equally ironic that when Kajsa changes from a pleasure-seeking creature to a person eager to share Tåbb's political interests, he rejects her in order to carry out his plan to die. In rejecting her he grasps for the strongest argument he can find and pretends to have been a strikebreaker, thus using a political rather than emotional reason to end her love for him, and she leaves him. This moment of dramatic irony is soon followed by the ultimate irony in Tåbb's existence.

The concept of Tåbb's "image of health" (135), his definition of a dignified existence, is replaced by ideas he previously would have regarded as unhealthy. Instead of finding the collective existence as a proletarian worker the only worthwhile life, Tåbb, nursed back to health in the hospital, demonstrates "a will to nurse individuality"

(239). He returns to his place of origin, and his dreams of a Marxist Garden of Eden are replaced by social democratic reformism and a garden in his own backyard.

IV *Humor*

While we may regard Tåbb's "manipulations" to eliminate conflicts between his life and his ideas with irony, we relate to him as a person with humor.[18] Humor, in Ahlin's sense of the word, Nielsen explains, means "loyalty to reality" expressed in acceptance of its joy *and* pain, including a will to "remain faithful to both these conditions of life, even though it may be tempting to escape from the tension they create."[19] Ahlin's humor resembles Luther's. Both men combine their notion of man as a mixture of sublime and ordinary qualities with a compassionate love of man even in his grotesque and ridiculous moments.[20] In his book *Humor, grotesk och pikaresk. Studier i Lars Ahlins realism (The Humorous Realism of Lars Ahlin)*, Hans-Göran Ekman provides an excellent analysis of Ahlin's concept of humor, which, Ekman argues, was inspired by Söderblom's Luther studies.[21]

Tåbb does not originally view his life with humor and is therefore unable to accept its undesirable elements; he must change them into desirable ones or be crushed by them. Sometimes he manages to reach a satisfying intellectual-ironical synthesis, as when he concludes that Christ is a strikebreaker. Another time, however, his suffering becomes unbearable and he gives in to his need to feel wanted instead of rejected. This happens when he meets Anna.

However, momentarily tempted to sink into blissful individualism after making love to Anna, Tåbb feels his confidence return and thinks that "his hatred of the impersonal was only due to a temporary confusion." Now again he "loved materialist existence . . . there was no real life apart from materialism" (101). His sexual happiness with Anna translates into political happiness, and he "loves" not her but materialism.

Gradually, he incorporates other words into his existence. He first articulates an attitude formed by humor when he listens to the words of the *Internationale*. He realizes then that ideologies encourage "manipulations" and invite compromises which are ultimately destructive in their disrespect of the present which constitutes his true existence: "How does it happen that we get so enthusiastic and optimistic about ideas of paradise and progress, he wondered. They are ultimately revealing. They actually pronounce a sentence over the present" (153). There should be a way to preserve individual dignity in the present. "Is there no peace for a conscientious person living in a period between capitalism and socialism?" (156) Tåbb wonders. And by introducing "between" as a positive concept of reality, he takes the first step toward accepting not only the extremes of existence but also all its variations. His ironical-intellectual attitude is gradually replaced by the analytical and yet tolerant and generous perspective on man which is characteristic of humor. In this process, existence acquires double characteristics. On the one hand he realizes that each person is confined to his specific conditions. But on the other, he sees man's social, political, and economic conditions to be only temporary compared to his more basically human qualities.[22]

First, however, his loss of faith in Marxism leaves him in a state of limbo. His old language does not fit into his new perspective on life, and he cannot yet articulate his changing awareness adequately. His lack of words for this new view of existence is illustrated in the episode with the salesman Andersson. Tåbb is taciturn; Andersson, verbose, embellishing his language with unique forms and compounds. Andersson too is dissatisfied with existence, but, unlike Tåbb who seeks for a viable form of existence, Andersson wants to create illusion. "He sought the incredible. . . . Words streamed incessantly from him with amazing ease. (He whipped up and counterfeited reality using the words as a beater.)" (162). Andersson, by his totally different approach to their common cause of discontent, provides a foil for Tåbb. Just as Ivar, the criminal, showed by contrast that Tåbb was not a dishonorable lumpenproletarian, Andersson, with his dishonest use of words makes Tåbb's lack of words seem a desirable quality, rather than a deficiency. Andersson's verbosity also provides a form of comic relief from Tåbb's speechless depression.

It is in his search for a new language that Tåbb finally learns to look upon himself with humor rather than irony. He accomplishes this after meeting two persons, each of whom represents one aspect of his old self. First he encounters an unemployed young man. They are much alike in their dreams about class solidarity, and in having had these dreams shattered by the narrow-minded materialistic individualism of the employed worker whose help they have been seeking. The young man, who once hit a man who boasted about being a strikebreaker, has now suffered so much that he could even become a strikebreaker himself. Still he feels degraded by this potential betrayal of his ideal and cries in despair. Then he confesses his dreams about going to school and becoming a spokesman for the working class and Tåbb recognizes himself in this distressed, and yet idealistic, young being. As a kind of sentimental gesture, Tåbb gives him money for school, hoping that at least he can be saved. Here Tåbb uses an emotional rather than intellectual justification for his action, thus indicating a shift toward humor in his perception of life.

In Staffan Hyrell, Tåbb finds his problems reflected intellectually, but in another "language" than his own. In a sweeping historical-intellectual survey, Staffan offers Lutheran and Freudian alternatives to Tåbb's Marxism. Pointing out that Lutheran reform is based on grammatical revelation,[23] and referring to Protagoras' rhetorical technique, which through a shift of point of view makes something bad seem better, Staffan succeeds in making Tåbb redefine his situation in a new "language."

Tåbb's alternative to the *Manifesto* centers around the concept to *die*, meaning "passage" in a mythical sense: initiation to adulthood, man's coming-of-age, accepting opposing and yet coexisting qualities in life and himself. Realizing that he must die and thereby, paradoxically, discovering a new perspective on life, Tåbb experiences a "merry" *(munter)* ecstasy. The word will be used in later novels to indicate the protagonist's humorous reaction to his situation. Humor is also present in Tåbb's changing attitude toward work which becomes more Lutheran than Marxist. He recognizes the value of work as such, "patient, insistent, everyday work" (239), and will in the future be guided by the principle of reformation rather than revolution.

CHAPTER 3

Death and Failure

I Definitions of death

THE concept of death is a recurring motif in Ahlin's work. Here
death is an aspect of failure in that when man sees himself as a
failure he is in a sense dead until some traumatic experience leads to
a death involving total reevaluation of self.[1] But the death of failure
may also lead to ultimate and final death. Ahlin's concept of death
seems to have been insired by Luther's discussion in *Lectures on
Romans*. Death is of two kinds, Luther says: "temporal death and
eternal death . . . which is also spiritual. Hence it [spiritual death] is
very often called a sleep, a rest, a slumber. Eternal death is also
twofold. The one kind is good, very good. It is the death of sin and
the death, by which the soul is released and separated from sin and
the body is separated from corruption and through grace and glory is
joined to the living God."[2] This eternal spiritual death, in other
words, liberates man from bondage to worldly concerns while he still
remains in the world, "present in all things with his sense."[3]

Also in Karl Barth's discussion of death in his *The Epistle to the
Romans* we find material useful for our understanding of Ahlin, and
we know that he studied both Luther and Barth during his formative
years. Barth's list of the features that bind man to this world is here
particularly interesting. Apart from basic needs such as hunger,
sleep, and sex, Barth says, man is bound by his "lusts," that is, the
sinfulness and corruption of his mortal body, the "longing to 'express myself,' my temperament, and my originality, my determina-
tion to know and to create, the blind passion of my will and finally,
and presumably supremely, my 'need of religion' with which is
linked a veritable macrocosm of social lusts."[4] When we are willing
to "be drowned in baptism," Barth argues using a phrase from
Luther, we in this death which is grace surrender all such lusts to

God.[5] Radically including all aspects of human activity Barth here most strongly condemns man's inclination to depend upon institutions and systems for his sense of identity and meaning. Ahlin is equally averse to social institutions which promote rankings and gradings of the individual and thereby violate his innermost being, which should stand independent of man-made evaluations.

This rejection of man's dependence on institutions and other worldly definitions of self emanates from Paul's discussion of death in his Epistle to the Romans, where death is said to be a power which liberates man from the law. Commenting on the relation between man and the law, Nygren in his *Commentary on Romans* states that the law's ability to "rule as man's lord" is eliminated by death which, then, has made us "dead to that which held us captive."[6] In this captivity, man is limited spiritually and therefore unable to perceive and receive God's grace, which is given regardless of merit and stands above the law which sees only merit. As long as man is dependent on the law or his social lusts for appreciation of self, he is contained in a "body of death"[7] which subjects him to an existence as a perishable object, to what Barth labels "thing-i-ness."[8] This leads to insecurity and spiritual misery.

Man will naturally try to escape this emotional torment and can do so either through a figurative death manifested in traumatic experience or change, or literal death by finishing his temporal life. However, figurative death on these grounds is different from a death into grace, Barth claims, and is therefore no permanent solution to man's despair: "Death is not grace so long as it is a merely relative negation, that is, so long as the attack upon the man of this world peters out in mere criticism of, opposition to or revolution against this or that concrete thing."[9] There must be a profound change of heart, the Kierkegaardian leap of faith, leaving behind all demands for temporal, rational, and personal reassurance of worthiness. This must occur before man can truly accept his self and die to the inescapable degrading inequalities of the world, and to its need for an intellectually perceived (logical) order established by man's will.

In the Christian notion of death there is an inherent contradiction of death bringing forth life: "He that findeth his life shall lose it and he that loseth his life for my sake shall find it" said Christ to his disciples before sending them off on their mission (Matt. 10:39). And the same dialectics of paradox are expressed in a secular context in Marx's statement that only through complete loss of man is it possible to accomplish complete rewinning of man.[10] The paradox articulates the duality of existence by challenging the conventions of systems and rationality. Constant through the variety of its definitions runs the concept of death as *change*. Death as change, then, is basically how we are to understand Ahlin's use of this concept. His characters may feel a need for change originating from their sense of failure, or they may enforce change as a consequence of their own sense of ideals. Ahlin's concept of death contains features from the Christian tradition as well as archetypal elements, as we will see in the following discussion of three novels utilizing these different connotations of death.

The first of these is *Min död är min (My Death Is My Own)*. Its place within the tradition of Lutheran theology as gleaned from a body of works with which Ahlin had come in contact during his formative years is brilliantly perceived by Hans-Göran Ekman in *Humor Grotesk och Pikaresk. Studier i Lars Ahlins realism (The Humorous Realism of Lars Ahlin)*.[11] Ahlin himself said about the novel that he wanted to "describe people who have failed, nothing else." He intended to "show how failure works inward and outward, which manipulations our psyche can perform to soothe the painful experience."[12]

II   My Death Is My Own

A   *The plot: The process of accepting one's self*

The novel is divided into three parts.[13] In the first part, "A gift of flesh and blood," we meet the two protagonists, Georg Sylvan, a traveling salesman, and Engla Käll, who does ironing and rents out rooms. A third protagonist, Olga, Sylvan's estranged wife, is present in spirit but she never materializes in person. Engla's rooms are rented by a group of circus artists, among them a hunchback, who is in fact a dwarf with an artificial hump. He knows that behind Engla's facade of a woman with strict morals and principles, there is a woman with strong sexual needs.

When Sylvan first enters Engla's kitchen, she, without looking at him, thinks he is the dwarf and treats him with repressed scorn. But when she discovers that Sylvan is Olga's husband, she becomes eager to please him. He has come because Olga, who lived with her lover at Engla's, told him there is a gift waiting for him there. He finds Engla's soliciting manners almost unbearable and she herself physically repulsive, and yet his curiosity about the gift makes him stay. Gradually realizing that the gift is Engla herself, he is disgusted. Rather than accept Engla as a replacement for Olga, he will drown himself in an ice hole, as he was planning to do at first. Yet he lingers in Engla's place for reasons he does not articulate and while there discovers that the dwarf's hump is artificial.

The dwarf's main interest in life is to play upon people's sexual needs. One of the circus people, Jacques, has been inspired by the dwarf to make love to the virgin Nineta, his dancing partner. The dwarf helps him to set the scene for the deflowering of Nineta. This will happen while Jacques and Nineta are practicing, watched by the dwarf through a crack in the wall. As he vicariously follows their every movement and fantasizes about the best moment for the great act, Engla enters the room. Simultaneously, to his great disappointment, the dwarf realizes that Jacques, stricken by the ethereal beauty of Nineta, has transformed his fleshly desires into solemn worship of her appearance and kneels submissively before her. Now Engla rips off his artificial hump and beats him hysterically until Sylvan enters and makes peace. The dwarf, his ridiculous self exposed, falls to the floor as if dead. While in this state of transitional consciousness he begins to create in his mind a new artistic act and thus escapes his degrading reality by becoming an artist.

Shortly thereafter Sylvan makes love to Engla, brutally taking out on her his shame at having failed as Olga's husband. He hates her trivial dreams about middle-class respectability in marriage, her spinster dreams as he calls them. By humiliating her sexually he wants her to realize that she is worthless, but in fact he only demonstrates his own lack of dignity.

The second part, "A trip to the beautiful birch tree," takes place during midsummer with a mixture of idyllic and grotesque elements, in a sense capturing the essence of Swedish midsummer celebrations. Sylvan and Engla are going to celebrate midsummer with their friends in the country. The company consists of an interesting group of odd characters from the lower strata of society, humorously depicted, resembling the characters in some of Steinbeck's novels, or Fellini's films. Sylvan organizes an adventurous birch collecting expedition for the children. Their mirth and excitement contrast with the distress and repressed passion among the adults. Sylvan, disgusted by Engla's too obviously displayed need for affection, touches her only occasionally. His caresses are given with such underlying scorn for her personal integrity that they turn into demeaning gestures.

Frustrated by his indifference, she strikes him and runs into the forest. She throws herself on the ground among lilies of the valley and screams obscenely to Sylvan who at that moment becomes nothing but a phallic force obliged to satisfy nature's demands almost against his will. Engla is here suddenly transformed from a pathetically unattractive woman begging awkwardly for Sylvan's love into a raging Fury of archetypal stature.

Afterward their relationship is different. For the first time, Sylvan openly admits his failure as Olga's husband and his feelings of humiliation. Speaking about his inner feelings he begins to love her in spite of her lack of attractive features. But this change within him is not immediately reflected in his actions. He assumes a mask of gaiety and clowns around among their friends as if nothing had happened.

The third part is called "My Death Is My Own." Back in town in the fall, Sylvan continues to surround himself with an odd group of people: a decayed journalist, an old candy lady, a couple of shady businessmen, and others. He tries to forget his own predicament by involving himself in these people's affairs, one more bizarre than the other.

Sylvan's most important undertaking is to help his friend Lagomrik marry Siri, a prostitute with four illegitimate children, who is at the moment confined to a "work institution." She will not agree to marry Lagomrik until Sylvan promises she will be featured in the newspapers as the heroine of a romantic escape from the institution. The description of the absurd negotiations with Siri conveys a Kierkegaardian disdain for flashy fame created by the press.

A young sculptor of little talent, Gösta, appears from nowhere and follows Sylvan wherever he goes. Gösta feels inferior and unsuccessful because his artistic gifts were not sufficient to make him an artist. He has only become a tombstone cutter and engraver. However, possessed by "widowpoisoning" he thinks that because he is a failure and as socially insignificant as the widow in Christ's parable he in a sense stands above the common man, just as Christ declared the poor widow's small contribution to be worth more than the larger sums of wealthier people.

Gösta talks about himself from time to time as he and Sylvan walk through the little community and meet Sylvan's bizarre friends. Gösta confesses that he finds comfort in the philosophy of reversed values or the "corruption of grace" as he reads the message in the parable about the widow. As he listens to Gösta, Sylvan gradually realizes that Olga had provided him with a false sense of value. We may say that he had in fact been "Olga poisoned," just as Gösta is "widowpoisoned." The poison had been something corrupt which prevented them from facing the truth about themselves and accepting themselves as failures.

This realization coincides with Siri's successful escape and a crowd of bizarre characters goes to celebrate at a hospital with the couple who are in charge of washing and disposing of the dead. They celebrate with drinks mixed from the alcohol intended for washing the dead.

Under the influence of the growing high spirit, Gösta suddenly understands that spiritual importance and social standing are not analogous. He realizes that grace is not a function of merit, whether genuine or acquired through a reversal of values. Through faith in Christ, he now accepts the world with all its misery. But this is only an escape from misery into the psychological comfort provided by religion.

Seeking a way to defile and destroy himself thoroughly and thus be liberated from the God who dulls his consciousness by giving him comfort, Gösta makes love to "Amanda with the Tumor," a decrepit and imbecile whore. He washes her tenderly and cuts her toe nails and then lies down with her and becomes sexually engulfed by her, as if eaten by a "viscous poisonous flower" (373). This rather repulsive scene is narrated as if the narrator were describing a sacred ritual. With a technique resembling Faulkner's, Ahlin here merges attraction with disgust. This scene was perhaps the one which Ahlin's contemporaries found most difficult to accept: "It is difficult to imagine anything more disgusting than the relationship between 'the boy' and the stinking imbecile Amanda with the Tumor. . . . One might ask what lies behind such a view of life. Chiefly it obviously reflects a gigantic fiasco for mankind demonstrated by World War II."[14]

Now, some thirty years and many fiascos later, the scene still remains one of the most powerfully conceived literary expressions for man's divided self, one part of him attracted to the realm of dark passion and degradation of self, the other longing for sacred beauty and harmony, free from the boundaries of the flesh. Today, after Beckett's and Genet's fictional world of decrepit creatures, Faulkner's evil characters and the black humor movement, the scene has to a large extent lost its shock value, while it has retained its symbolic value.

In his intercourse with Amanda, Gösta performs a sacred act with a most profane person, trying to reconcile himself to accept the ugly and the beautiful, to accept man as both sinner and saint. When he wakes up, he believes he has failed because his religion is intact. "In fact he had now reached a bottom of sorts," (373) the narrator informs us, and Gösta sits down to write his first poem (the only one published by Ahlin). Simultaneously with these events Sylvan finds that he can accept his love for Engla and live knowing he is a failure.

B Death of illusions

Sylvan's image of self is based on a lie. He sees himself as the happy husband of Olga. Therefore, when she eloped with her lover he had to face his lie which threw him into a crisis. Unlike Ibsen's doctor Relling, who advocates that man's life-lie must not be taken from him, Ahlin argues that man must not become so dependent on his ideal image of self that his sense of dignity rests on lies. Man must face the truth about his inadequacies. Ahlin regards man's inclination to dream of happiness in an ideal existence, which for Tåbb lies in the future and for Sylvan in the past, as ultimately destructive because it degrades man in his present life. Sylvan's wish to drown in an ice hole originates, therefore, less from a need to end a miserable existence than from a need to recapture an illusion of happiness.

But as he lies in Engla's little room, which reminds him of an ice hole with its pale green walls and a thin blood-red line across them, he must admit to himself that he had known the truth about his life all the time. His earlier experience in an ice hole taught him that his power of self deception then had been strong enough to prevail even in the hour of death:

> Why had he struggled so violently to save his life? It was not because he had felt stronger than ever the Olga and the children necessarily and happily belonged to him. No, his further thinking had not retained this feeling. He had failed, hadn't he. Completely! His love life and his family life had always been failures . . . that he had known from the beginning.
>
> But what had given him the strength? Soon he understood: It came from his despair at having failed so completely . . . then he still hoped day by day that he would succeed at last. As long as he did not despair. He must work and not give up. (21)

Even now as he tacitly confesses that his ideal image of self in the past was false, he believes that he will be able to return to his state of blissful self-deceit as long as he finds the right ice hole and the right situation. When he jumps into that hole he will die with respect for himself. But Sylvan must instead learn to confront his "afterward," Birgitta Trotzig points out, and accept an existence with both desirable and undesirable elements.[15]

Sylvan is unwilling to acknowledge undesirable elements because he is, like man in general, cursed with a compulsion to choose. Man's act of choosing, Ahlin claims, is also an act of evaluation and limits his perspective on life by seducing him into a life of illusions and dreams.[16] A person's illusions of worth are based upon his relationship with someone he perceives as superior. Sylvan defines himself only in relation to Olga who stands above him as an ideal for the image he wants to project. He is unable to reverse the process and create worth for himself in a relationship with someone he sees as inferior. Therefore he cannot accept the unattractive and insecure Engla as a replacement for Olga.

While Sylvan is people-oriented in his concept of self, he finds his value in being *Olga's* husband; Engla, who is socially oriented, finds her value in the *institution* of marriage. The roles chosen by them to define their worth have no absolute quality. Sylvan is in fact a cuckold husband and, paradoxically, prefers this rather ridiculous identity as long as it gives him a dignity within his frame of reference. Engla is a hard working, self-supporting woman, essentially moral in spite of having two illegitimate children, and yet she accepts demeaning treatment from Sylvan because through him she hopes to attain social respectability in marriage. Their ideals are arbitrarily chosen and ultimately destructive because they force Sylvan and Engla to sacrifice their personal integrity in order to satisfy their notion of worth. Paradoxically, in finding his worth as Olga's cuckold husband, Sylvan lost it; by losing this worth after the midsummer night's sexual adventure among the lilies he finds his worth in love.

Sylvan no longer clings to his illusions about his past, and finds himself behind the mask of his ideal self: "Sylvan's 'I' had become untied and lost its form in the present. Instead, it was stretched out in time like a channel with one opening to the past and another turned to a forum which perhaps was God or perhaps only his inner evaluations that had become substantiated in a *You* so that he could speak to it" (192). Directing his speech to Engla, she becomes his "*Thou*" in Buber's sense of the word, though he does not yet accept her completely as a *Thou* for his *I*. He confesses to Engla his shame at being a failure in his marriage but does not listen to her attempts to open a dialogue between them. Having disposed of his illusions he is first in an emotional limbo: "I will not be able to feel anything. I will only feel the pain of not feeling anything" (195). Engla's attitude toward him changes as she sees his profound despair. She now sees him not merely as someone to satisfy her sexually and provide her with middle-class respectability, but as a human being suffering like herself.

Their awareness of the other as a *Thou* is mutual, but more articulated by Engla at this point. She, like Anna in *Tåbb with the Manifesto*, seems to recognize that sharing equality in shame is a more intimate token of togetherness than any social bonds: "For the first time she felt Sylvan within her. . . . From now on he was going to be present in her and satisfy her also when he was absent" (196). Her love, from having been a function of social and physical needs, has been transformed into an expression of unlimited and unconditional love and has become more like Christian love than socioromantic love; it is no longer a function of social lust.

Simultaneously Sylvan changes his attitude toward her. He now loves her by virtue of the workings of *caritas infusa* (197). This phenomenon, as described by Nygren in *Eros and Agape*, is the result of the working of God's grace in man, and it liberates man from earthly desires and values to make him instead receptive to God's love.[17] For Sylvan it signifies his liberation from a need to seek values in the loved person, his need to love an object which will give him a sense of worth through its desirability. But he finds it impossible to accept this love for Engla: "At the same time he perceived this love to be so absolutely impossible that it could not make him act. That he would love this woman such as she was, so ridiculous, so full of prejudices, so void of all charm. No! This was too much" (197). He does not know that the night has changed her as well. When he wants to insult her by arranging for a double wedding with Lagomrik and his prostitute Siri, instead of being insulted she helps him organize Siri's escape. And shortly after his failure to demean her, he is again seized by the same inexplicable feeling of love as during the midsummer night.

At the drinking feast in the hospital's department for the dead, Sylvan finally overcomes his reservations about loving Engla. This happens in a scene typical of Ahlin in its mixture of sacred and profane elements: Sylvan, too drunk to stand on his feet, crawls over

to Engla and caresses her. Fantasizing about Olga and her lover in
the role of Christ and his disciples about to cross a lake, he whispers:
"Here is the boy Tor whom she seduced and he says before he steps
into Olga's boat 'Ought I not first bury your abandoned husband?'
'No,' she answers, 'He is dead to us but I'll give him a gift of flesh
and blood, a woman. Engla is her name and she is also dead. Let the
dead bury their dead'" (367 - 68). Sylvan is now free from his
degrading dependence on Olga; he is dead for her and from her.[18]
Walking toward Engla's house he continues to speak about their
happiness which will grow from accepting oneself even in decay and
disgust. They will leave all demeaning principles of comparison
behind and embrace all of existence with love, unconcerned with
merits or rank. Speaking and preaching, Sylvan walks upstairs with
Engla step by step:

And I believed I would never dare to love you, he whispered. I stood there
in all my failure. And Olga's shadow fell over me from behind and in front
of me sat all your spinster dreams like a red rag. I did not understand then
that my death is my own. I may have failed, so what. I want to bury you and
me. An enormous joy was left. Oh, to love that which decays and falls apart.
To decay and fall apart yourself, beloved. (377)

In spite of the differences, the successful ones and the failures belong
together, they always describe each other just as the carcass and the carcass
fly describe each other. Neither have a substance, a form, a face, an existence lacking its partner. . . (378 - 79)

— But we? whispered Engla, pressing her face to his chest.
— We whisper in each other's ears and into our hearts: My death is my own.
We will from now on always experience the joy of the dead: to bury each
other, to decay together piece by piece, to love your wounds, you loving
mine. (379)

Sylvan has at the end substituted, Melberg argues, "the societal
terms of failure for the existential ones of decay," and has rendered
insignificant societally established orders and comparisons, but he
does so without eliminating them. Sylvan accepts his conditions and
finds a new way of life without rejecting or denying his former life
ideals. He can now allow for two different perspectives on himself to
coexist and views himself humorously.[19]

C Escape from death

The dwarf and Gösta function partly as personifications of psychological elements in Engla and Sylvan respectively, and partly as

independent characters.[20] They demonstrate two kinds of escape from the pain of failure: escape into art and into religion. In "Reflexioner och utkast" ("Reflections and Outlines"), Ahlin calls their kinds of escapist the "creators and the fanatics, people intoxicated by individuality" *(egenartsberusad)*.[21]

The inspiration to use a dwarf as a character came, Lennart Göthberg relates, after Ahlin had read Lagerkvist's *The Dwarf*, published the year before Ahlin's novel. Göthberg had lent Ahlin a copy of *The Dwarf*, which he sat up all night reading. In the early morning an upset Ahlin exclaimed: "How in the world did Pär Lagerkvist do such a bad job of such a magnificent subject. . . . I'll present a completely different dwarf in my next novel . . . immensely superior."[22] Superior or not, Ahlin's dwarf is different from Lagerkvist's. The dwarf in Lagerkvist's novel is totally evil and sterile, he represents man's shadow in Jungian terms, while Ahlin's figure is mean and ridiculous without the metaphysical dimension of Lagerkvist's character.[23]

In the beginning, the dwarf symbolizes Engla's sexual guilt feelings. His life is centered around perverted or repressed sexual activities. He spends most of the day in a café selling wood sculptures of a man with a gigantic penis springing up at the push of a hidden button. He dreams about watching Jacques deflower Nineta, and he delights in making Engla watch the nude Jacques from the hidden crack in his wall. Furthermore, it is implied that he is himself impotent (his nose looks like a "shrivelled rubber tube" and "a boy's penis")[24] and therefore reduced to satisfying his own sexual needs through voyeurism. When Sylvan settles at Engla's place, he provides her with a legitimate outlet for her sexual needs and eliminates her need for the dwarf's offerings. This psychological change is illustrated in action, Nielsen points out, by the fact that Sylvan tells Engla about the artificial hump.[25] By informing Engla of the dwarf's secret shame, he destroys the dwarf's power over Engla which was dependent on his being able to play on Engla's sense of shame.

Twice a failure, first as a dwarf because he was not little enough to be interesting as a dwarf, then as a hunchback whose disguise was ignominiously revealed, the dwarf escapes his degradation through artistic imagination. In so doing he has derived "merit from his very shame, a liberating strength from his very defeat" (91). "Oh ecstacy from my misery" (92), he finally exclaims and falls asleep. When he thus elevates his misery to a higher experience, to art, we understand that his death brings about only psychological, not spiritual, change.

Gösta, in the earlier edition simply called "the boy," is Sylvan's shadow, psychologically speaking as well as literally; he follows him around like a shadow. Gösta lost his dignity when he was declared inadequate as an artist and reduced to a tombstone cutter, lowest in the artistic hierarchy. He has recaptured a sense of dignity by cling- ing to the "cross" of consolation provided by the reversal of hierarchies in Christ's parables of the widow and the children: the smallest will be the greatest. But even though he understands that this attitude is an escape from his failure rather than a transforma- tion of self, he finds the consolation offered in the parables ir- resistably appealing. He has become addicted to it like a drug, poisoned: "When I saw the widows, I discovered I was myself a widow, whispered the boy in a soft hallucinatory voice, and he slanted his arms in an imperfect gesture of crucifixion. I am the widow nailed to the cross! I am the widow . . ." (227).

Similarly, Sylvan is addicted to escapism from his own failure. He had stayed with Olga though she cheated on him because he had chosen her as a sign of his success: "Maybe I stayed only because I got it into my head that if I'm going to succeed in this life I must succeed with her. Then I became a sort of drug addict. . . . Olga herself and her skillful games were my poison, the drug I indulged in and soon could not be without" (39). When she left him, he in- dulged in dreams about restoring his dignity in the ice hole. His thoughts of drowning are hammering like incantations in his head throughout the first part of the novel, just as Gösta's fascination with the widow philosophy resounds throughout the third part. This structural analogy between them reinforces the psychological similarity developed in the third part.

Sylvan recognizes in Gösta qualities and attitudes he does not want to ascribe to himself, though the reader has no problems in see- ing how they mirror each other. Gösta found religion a *reversal* of ideals which satisfies his injured ego, and Sylvan wanted to escape into death to console his ego through a *return* to ideals. Both reject the present world and prefer illusions. But Sylvan is moving toward a more honest and humorous acceptance of self. He rejects failure only in relation to himself, and he helps and consoles his friends, who are all failures. This means that even when he cannot yet accept himself as a failure, he can embrace the notion of failure humorously and in his friends distinguish between human value and human ac- complishment.

During the party in the hospital's basement next door to the dead, Sylvan liberates himself from the boy and the kind of negative death he represents. The tension between them grows as Sylvan reacts with disgust to the boy's escapism. Gösta in turn becomes increasingly upset over Sylvan's refusal to share his escape into religion and find a Savior to comfort him in this world. First Sylvan smirks when the boy confesses to him that his inhibitions have fallen, and he now feels competent to spread his message; he is happy about being "an insignificant carrier of a great message. . . . What did I guess? Sylvan thought. . . . Now he builds up his own value in reverse (*Nu utkorar han sig bakvägen*)" (359), exactly what Sylvan himself was going to do in his ice hole: "I'll never forget the ice, he thought. When you cannot live with dignity is it then not most dignified to go to an ice hole and jump in without a sound. From sheer politeness, from sheer respect for oneself and life?" (69).

Gösta continues his preaching and confession in a rambunctious sermon about order and corruption, leading up to his reason for accepting Christianity. Though he recognizes a "polemic irony" (366) in Christ's words, he cannot embrace his own dual identity as sinner *and* saint. Consequently, in following Christ he is only following the "God of the widow" (*änkeguden*) who reverses the hierarchies of this world. His consciousness does not become radical enough to embrace the notion of total elimination of hierarchies which takes place in spiritual death.

When Sylvan liberates himself from all of the world's notion of values and orders by declaring that "my death is my own," the boy finds this adoption of void terrifying as a viable principle. "— Do you love your death, though you know it is death you love, the boy whispered. But he raised his voice at once and said accusingly: — It is disgraceful! It is the most disgraceful way of all!" (368). Why "disgraceful" if not for the boy's apprehension about the function of religion as a supreme and inviolable principle, which he feels is being attacked by Sylvan's absolute rejection of all principles? The boy uses religion to reconcile himself with this world. Not blessed with the gift of humor, [26] Gösta needs religion to escape, psychologically, into temporal comfort. He is unable to live without illusions. After making love to "Amanda with the Tumor," he seems to have reached the lowest point of his existence beyond which he might be cut off from his religion, which will "burst whatever life I possess" (374). But he will not be totally liberated through spiritual death, like Sylvan. At this moment of potential liberation he writes his first poem and, like the dwarf, transforms his misery into ecstacy. He escapes or dies into art.

III   Pious Murders

A   *Introduction*

"Pious" means "idealistic" in Ahlinian lingua, as Erik Hjalmar Linder explains in "Guds pennfäktare. Lars Ahlin och livsdilemmat ("God's Pen Crusaders. Lars Ahlin and Life's Dilemma").[27] Pious people, like idealistic people, perceive the world narrowly and give it a simple consistency it can never attain.[28] Piety and idealism are destructive because they victimize man. Yet man seems to need this objectification of self, since he usually clings to some kind of belief in an unambiguous world instead of accepting the inexplicable dualism of the actual world. Ahlin sees this inclination of man as his "most devastating and problematic quality."[29] Man makes himself an instrument upon which his ideal may play, be it economic, political, moral, or religious. He loses his sense of humanness in the process of obeying the laws of the ideal. But man, Ahlin believes, is a being of contradictory identities which are reconcilable in this world through paradox and humor, and become eliminated in the next world by God's grace.

Ingmar Bergman formulates a similar and equally negative opinion about idealism in *The Seventh Seal* (1956) when the squire tells the painter about the Crusades: "For ten years we sat in the Holy Land and let snakes bite, flies sting us, wild animals eat us, heathens butcher us, the wine poison us, the women give us lice, the lice devour us, the fevers rot us, all for the Glory of God. Our crusade was such madness that only a real idealist could have thought it up."[30] Piety destroys man's sense of perspective. The knight stays away for ten years, forsaking his wife and estate in the absurd belief that he will serve God better by submitting himself to the indignities of the crusade than to toil in everyday work.

Likewise, a "pious" person in Ahlin's work is someone who thinks his commitment to a cause liberates him from his duties to his fellow man and from his involvement with worldly, even though trivial, human matters.[31] But since his ideals are man-made, he is only tying himself to the world while he thinks he is standing above it. Ruled by ideals rather than faith, the pious have replaced God's righteousness with self-righteousness.

Pious Murders is one of Ahlin's more intricately structured novels. In his study of the novel, Erik A. Nielsen chose to follow the psychological relationship between the characters and to analyze Ahlin's language, which adds new meanings and connotations to many words, "pious murder" being the most conspicuous but not the only innovation. Nielsen also comments on the narrative structure, seeing the novel's fragmented form as an illustration of the protagonist's isolation, his inability to communicate. The novel is based on a kind of diary fiction, Nielsen observes, and is "composed from writings Aron left after his death and comments on the text." We discover "three time levels in the composition: (1) Aron's past, (2) his present, and (3) the editor's reminiscences as he edits the material." Each chapter consists of two or more elements; there are "shifts from one time to another and between narration and analytical-philosophical sections."[32]

Arne Melberg focuses on the dialectical pattern of the structure, which he sees in the play between "the epic now-level" and Aron's or other characters' memories and in the moves between what Aron "has written" or "was going to write."[33] Each point of view, it should be added, is determined by the structurally omniscient narrator-editor's position in epic present. He also discusses the dialectical tension between "inner" man, man's spiritual existence, and "outer" man, man's societal existence.

Nielsen explains the artistic unity in this complex work by bringing various motifs together thematically. First he analyzes "Aron's world," then four main streams of events, two erotic, two political, and finally the meaning of "A death in piety." In the following account we learn how the thematic elements are incorporated in the sequential pattern of the novel, an approach intended to complement Nielsen's analysis of the thematic interrelationship.

B The plot: The failure of good intentions

Aron has returned to his home town with the intention of beginning a new life from an escape into art.[34] He wants to replace his self-centered "will" with "sense," that is, unquestioned acceptance of "truth" and multifarious nature uncorrupted by culture. To be able to do so he must put order into his life, he believes, by defining himself in relation to the past and the future. For this reason he wants to put a tombstone on his father's grave and marry Evangeline. He also wants to create true relationships by establishing a dialogue between himself and others. He explains his motives for coming back to his friend Roland in a series of observations on the nature of grammar and on man's innermost being. Sometimes he giggles in the middle of his serious and intriguing discourse, as if the situation were too absurd.

This happens when he realizes that his philosophical and deeply felt monologue is delivered to Roland's indifferent and uncomprehending ear. He perceives the irony between their failure to communicate and their performance of communication in their speaker-listener relationship. In addition, Aron's emotional mood clashes with his formal language and makes the whole situation comical. Aron will giggle many times throughout the novel as he senses similar discrepancies between form and content of experience. Had he been able to incorporate this sense of being, he would have been able to live humorously, embracing the dualism of existence. But his giggling only means that he perceives the irony of life, not that he can live it with humor.

Agnes, Roland's mistress who loves Aron, sneaks up on them, delighted to see Aron back. She makes Aron dance with her and tries to seduce him. This evokes in him memories of her mother, the prostitute Greta, who was murdered by one of her clients. Aron remembers how eagerly Greta had wanted him to kiss her mouth, something her customers did rarely, if ever. The men reserved their mouth for their wives and fiancées, Greta had told him, thereby preserving a sense of pure love for the beloved, while they performed the *act* of love with her. By making the kiss a token of esteem and then withholding it, Greta's customers had long been degrading her, not by what they did, but, ironically, by what they did not do.

Desperately trying to gain a sense of respectability and dignity, she had, Aron speculates, forced her last customer to kiss her. But in so doing she violated his sacred territory and defiled him, and therefore he had to kill her in an act of pious murder, thus demonstrating that the pious feel no compassion or understanding for values outside their own limited frame of reference. The story about Greta teaches the Lutheran belief that the ultimate value of an act lies in the heart, not in the act itself. Nevertheless, Aron agrees to satisfy Agnes by making love to her even though he loves Evangeline.

The following day he receives a letter from Roland suggesting that he join Roland and Agnes on a trip to Italy, explaining that there is no sense in their going without him because Agnes loves him. Roland does not know whom he loves, Agnes or Aron, or maybe Agnes in Aron. He believes that Agnes, by loving Aron, has implanted in his being her very "person" which Roland therefore can reach only by relating to Aron intimately. Soon Roland enters Aron's room, giggling and moving like a girl, trying by his behavior to make Aron forget he is a man and make love to him. In this way Roland believes he may be able to retrieve Agnes' innermost "person." To a somewhat confused Aron, Roland explains how Agnes is divided into two elements: love placed within Aron and lust experienced with Roland. He thinks that Agnes, who has aborted two pregnancies for lack of a sense of inner unity between her lust and her love, now is pregnant again. He hopes that with Aron present, she may find a way to unite love and lust and so be able to give birth. When Aron tries to escape Roland and goes to church, Roland follows him in a mask.

After the church visit Aron, still followed by Roland, goes to a café where he sees Dora, a cleaning woman who divides her life between being a political worker within the labor party and being a Christian. She keeps her two identities separate because her political friends believe them to be incompatible. While they talk, Roland sends him a note telling about Agnes and Lilly, a woman Aron once made love to. After Aron's intercourse with Lilly, Roland explains, her lust was implanted with Aron and therefore she lives in a sexless marriage with Sven. Agnes and Lilly are both incomplete without Aron, Roland continues, and try to find wholeness from each other instead; Lilly, dressed in pants, visits Agnes at night to talk about Aron.

While Roland sends these notes to Aron, Dora explains that she does not like Christians as a group, because: "They think you attack their person when you attack their superficial piety and conservativism" (63). Such a narrow preoccupation with self is illustrated in a secular sense by Berglund. He is a former member of the *Riksdag* now writing countless editorials. His piety is to be a missionary of birth control information among the workers. Consequently, he has refused to impregnate his wife.

Leaving the café, Aron is picked up by Agnes in a cab and Roland soon joins them. The cab ride makes Aron reminisce about his first car ride. He had once been kidnapped by a young woman. She brought him to a forest and threatened him with a gun, but soon pleads that he kill her with the same gun which, it turned out, was a toy gun. In fact, she wanted Aron to scratch her back with a twig from a spruce, and he had done so until she fell asleep. On his way back to the village Aron had stumbled upon a sleeping man, a mass murderer sought by the whole community.

Aron had begun to scratch him lightly with a twig and saw, reflected in his body, images of joy and pleasure and tender love of self. He had been filled with a wonderful sensation about the double nature of man: the murderer in his sleep is simply a being without connection to human and societal relations. Elated, Aron cries out: "So you are also blessed" (84) (with a life outside value systems, that is). The murderer wakes up and, returned to the world of the law, he runs off. Aron's words had led the murderer away from "his physical consciousness to an intellectual-linguistic consciousness with its moralistic evaluation." The language gave him his social value[35] just as it gave Tåbb his.

As soon as Aron's memories from the forest have been told we are brought back to the present with Agnes and Aron walking into a forest, whereupon Agnes begins to undress. She lusts for him, hoping that her lust may be able to unite with her love which he already possesses. She thinks that if she succeeds, this will give her a sense of unity. Aron agrees to make love to her but talks about Evangeline who gave her body to her work because she did not dare to commit herself to love. Evangeline had been unable to accept within herself both an Eros principle striving up *from* the world and her body striving *in* the world. Therefore she had chosen to work in the world and renounce love. Evangeline, thinking she can find love, or God, only away from the world believes, like the people of Babel, that God does not exist in this world, but is found only in celestial heights. But God is not exclusive, Aron says, but loyal to everyone and is with us here on this earth.

Presumptuously, Aron also tries to be loyal to everyone when Lilly suddenly appears, undresses, and throws herself on top of him and Agnes. Aron is about to make love to her too when Roland comes, followed by Dora and separates them in spite of Aron's protests: "Loyal to everyone," Aron yells, "Idiot, whispered Dora, look how silly things get when you think you're in heaven though you're still on the earth" (91). She takes Aron away from the bizarre foursome affair to bring him to Berglund, the man who is loyal only to himself.

On his way to Berglund, Aron speculates about the nature of truth, language, and art. He talks to Berglund about the past, about fights between workers and capitalism, and about clashes between men's need for irresponsibility and preservation of dignity, and women's instinct for preservation of life in all embracing love and care of children. Then Aron leaves to go to his father's grave.

Arriving at the church yard he discovers to his embarrassment that he cannot pay for the cab. The capitalist Brinkman, who is visiting the grave of his old nurse and substitute mother, helps him out. As they talk about Brinkman's past Aron remembers his father, whom the narrator merges gradually with Brinkman in a process described almost like a ritual:

Thus Aron thought: I am standing on ice crashing
into stars.
Thus Brinkman thought: I am yearning for ice crashing
into stars.
Thus Aron thought: Acropolis was my father's favorite
name.
Thus Brinkman thought: Acropolis is yearning for
ice crashing into stars.   (121)

Brinkman, who has successfully amassed money and property, now wants to die beautifully, like an old couple who had ventured out on thin ice in their yearning for fresh milk. The ice had crashed into a star, opened up, and swallowed their bodies. The beauty of their death lies in the purpose of action, Brinkman explains:

Everything these people carried within themselves died, their bodies died, nothing of them was left; they disappeared completely in the black star of water. And such is all life. Death takes everything. If we are only to buy a bar of soap we are totally present when we buy the bar of soap. If we die while buying the soap all that is us dies. But to die while on a beautiful errand, to die on an errand of yearning for milk is a beautiful death. To die with truth on your lips is most beautiful of all.   (124)

Ahlin's belief in the equal value of all that life offers, whether trivial or sublime, is here most powerfully expressed, as is the meaning of action. Each action, like every kind of work, is ultimately our most meaningful undertaking because we can die any time during that act. The importance of death overshadows everything else. In the sincerity with which we encounter death, and consequently life, lies our primary value.

When Aron wakes up the next day, his trivial morning activities, getting up, washing, exercising, looking at his face in the mirror, are mixed with speculations on God and faith: "He did not find the life of faith in his life. He could not pray. Therefore no sinner or righteous person was made from him. God was neither wrath nor love in his conscience. Aron cannot say: my God. Here is Aron. Here is his word: God. Now he thinks he is damned" (127). He is damned because he has made God a Buberian *It* when God should be *Thou*. He is damned also because he strives for the impossible: to satisfy all demands put on him. He is beginning to experience how difficult it is to obey the law, here represented by growing demands on his attention and time. Eager to answer all calls upon him, he has not yet accomplished his original task: to put a stone on his father's grave.

He meets Lilly who demands that he return her lust and, having failed to arouse his lust and thereby recapture her own, she first tries to shoot him. Then she gives him a large sum of money in a purse. The money is his, she says, but the purse is not. When he subsequently returns a minor sum in exchange for the purse, Lilly feels released from her bonds to Aron. She has given him money, symbolizing her lust, and he has returned part of what she gave him. He has thereby returned the same thing he got from her. He retains part of the money as a symbol that she is buying herself free.

Their spiritual-emotional relationship has in this procedure been translated into a substance which can be handled concretely and rationally. When man is thus dealt with as if he were a thing, the principle of justice is violated; man as a person is replaced by man as an object, in a process called *reification* or *objectivation*.[37] There is no other way for them to deal with their relationship, since they are trapped in their need to seek rational meaning instead of accepting irrational nature.

During most of the bargaining with Lilly, Aron is making love to a cleaning woman in a rocking chair because she has asked him to impregnate her. After these bizarre interactions with the two women, Aron goes to see Berglund again.

Berglund, unlike Aron, has not obeyed demands for impregnation. They are alike however, in that they share the reasons for their actions: piously, they are victims of their ideal image of self. Berglund identifies himself as a promoter of causes, as a sociopolitical being. Aron strives to be all-loving, satisfying everybody.

Aron has coffee with Berglund, Inga, and Dora and during this simple act, Inga delivers an important message to Berglund: "I respect and esteem your idealism," she says, "but why did you not give me a child?" (157). Then she tells him that she is pregnant by another man, Larsson. But she still wants to take care of Berglund and asks him to come and live with Larsson and her. Berglund rejects her offer because he cannot leave his work in town, his editorials, and his politics. Inga then looks deeply into his eyes, clasps his hand happily, and leaves him.

After this exposure to unconsumed love sacrificed to ideals, Aron goes to see Evangeline. Their reunion releases a string of poetic lines describing their love in terms reflecting the love of Inga's gestures when she leaves Berglund:

— Beloved, my hand has never forgotten your hand.
— My glance has never forgotten the peace in your glance.
— Never the journey upward.
— Never love's creation of light in light. (172)

Their love is encased in marble, beautiful, classical perfection, but removed from daily life and its trivial activities, divorced from man's striving for social satisfaction. Evangeline is afraid that loving Aron will create an extreme tension from which ultimately her social being, defined as "busy ants" in her, will crack her love, the beautiful marble. She sees no way to find harmony between the extremes or to let them coexist in life. Therefore she asks Aron to "save" her into a life in Eros: "— Everything is different if only our eyes unite. Then you are no longer you. I no longer I. In Eros he is no longer he, she no longer she. . . . There is no submission and no superiority. There everything is new" (178).

Evangeline's consciousness is fragmented because her sense of Eros, love lifting her up from the world, is incompatible with her existence as a physical being. Therefore, the ecstacy of love in her mind lies in union of eyes, in spirit only. She is in despair and believes that she will find peace only in death, but she will now once more try to bring together love and self and make love to Aron, and so unite body and spirit. But she fails, and dies instead.

Aron's plan to marry Evangeline is destroyed by her death and he feels "thrown into war," that is, in a situation ruled by no laws and without order. At this point Roland comes to him and wants to exchange the money Lilly gave Aron for a sum ten times larger. This exchange will finally bring Agnes and Roland's relationship in balance, he believes, because through Lilly the money has become a substantiation of lust and love in Aron. By acquiring this particular money, Roland will consequently be in control both of the desire (coming from Lilly's part) and the love (being Agnes' bond with Aron) within Aron and so be able to possess Agnes completely. Aron insists, however, on returning the money directly to Agnes, whereupon they all meet and drive to Berglund's place.

Berglund suffers because Inga has left him. A meeting is now called to discuss the nature of his suffering, whether it is sociopolitical or "special," that is, exclusive and personal. Aron is chosen to take the minutes. Berglund's emotions are going to be discussed and properly documented in a formal way, in grotesque contrast to the mood of his problem and his despair. Aron suddenly comes up with a practical solution to Berglund's problem: "If you are out of money, I can lend you some. I mean if you want to take a cab to Inga and Larsson" (208); Berglund's suffering then stops, and the meeting dissolves.

Leaving the meeting Aron is surrounded by all his friends, each demanding his attention and company. Confused, he giggles and leaves them after having laced and unlaced somebody's boots several times in exchange for a photo of Evangeline which he does not get anyway. His involvement with others becomes more and more bizarre and nonsensical. His handwork does not give him that which his heart desires because his activities are meaningless repetitions, services without purpose.

Interrupted by Lilly and Sven, he leaves the house and meets Brinkman, whose ruthless gathering of wealth and power will lose its meaning unless he can change his guilt to innocence in his moment of death.

Brinkman wants to go to another town immediately with Aron, and as an incentive for him to come along he tells Aron that he is going to inherit his fortune. Agnes helps Aron pack and explains that she got the idea to liberate herself from Aron through money from the parable about the good Samaritan: The Samaritan, unable to care for the beaten man himself, gave money to those who were to replace him in doing so. Money then came to serve as his substitute. By analogy, Agnes thought that she could substitute her love within Aron for money.

With this kind of thinking Brinkman, ironically, also becomes a substitute Samaritan because he has constantly substituted money for personal relations and love. His dependence on money for this purpose illustrates his reification of human relations, his piety.[38] Having treated others as objects his whole life, he now wants to make himself an object. He wants to be murdered and thereby gain his death as a victim, to substitute his guilt for the reification of himself.[39] Later he falls into a river and drowns but it is unclear whether he fell or Aron pushed him.

Several days later, Lilly and Sven with Roland and Agnes celebrate Brinkman's death, which had liberated them from undefined bonds. Though their behavior seems identical in Aron's eyes, the narrator defines Lilly and Sven's actions as "pious," Roland and Agnes' as "profane." Aron's four friends here personify his own spiritual confusion: what is the true nature of his actions? How will he be able to make sense of the world, divided as it is into elements looking alike and yet having different names? Do words in fact describe the true quality of people and their actions?

They decide to have a picnic by a swamp. Singing and joking they proceed toward a suitable place, each carrying something; Aron carries his briefcase handed him by Roland who had taken it away from him earlier. Underneath the friendly surface there is a sense of hostility toward Aron. A power game between him and the others is taking place, but he seems unaware of the significance of their gestures and words. He does only what he is told to do and remains nearly silent.

Arriving at the swamp, Roland takes out the tombstone, lets it fall in front of Aron's feet and asks him to step on it. Sven and Roland then tie Aron to the stone and prepare to carry him out into the swamp while Agnes and Lilly follow them giggling. They leave Aron tied to the stone in the middle of the swamp, where he slowly sinks while the others eat, drink, and sing.

When they at last decide to leave, Aron refuses to obey Roland's command that he bend down and untie the ropes. He seems petrified, looking like a statue half sunken in the swamp. The others return to society, to their everyday lives but "Aron had fallen on his face in the water. He never raised his body again" (292). And so ended Aron's return to his hometown.

C Death without grace

Unlike Tåbb, Aron had not tied his sense of failure to a particular social identity, but to personal relationships. He had left the community struck by "dumbness," incapable of communicating, living in a sense of void or disorder. Now he is returning to bring order which, he thinks, is a matter of establishing proper relations; he will place a stone on his father's grave and thereby put the past in proper perspective by symbolically dividing the world into the realm of the spirit (the dead) and that of the body (the living). At the same time this division will permit the realms to coexist. He will also begin to "respond to addresses," that is, to relate to others in dialogues, thereby accepting the dualism of existence. We soon realize, however, that most of Aron's verbal communications are monologues, whether spoken, written, or thought.

Aron speaks of replacing his "thoughts of will" with "thoughts of sense." We may understand this to mean, in Barthian terms, that Aron is corrupted by social lusts; his thoughts of will demand a comprehension of life on man's terms instead of God's. Now he is striving for a new awareness, his "thoughts of sense," which will accept separation between man's world and God's, between man in his social role and man in his Christian identity. As Aron sits talking to Roland in the beginning he understands, however, that he is destined to remain in his "thoughts of will," held prisoner by persons from his past: "I would never obtain a liberated future. The thoughts of sense were never to be thought by me. My destiny was to think the thought of will and to enter into preserving the past. Those who had once heard my voice and felt my hands wanted to use me. When are you going to execute me, God?" (16). The answer soon comes: when his friends do not need him any more.

His four friends want him to rescue them from their incomplete lives. Only he can do it because he possesses the elements missing in them, in their lives, and they demand that he revoke their misery, even though it means that he neglect his own mission. They demand from him, in other words, the services of a Savior, and Aron consents to serve them because he believes he can help them restore order in their world and so also in his. Ironically, he sees his dealings with them as dialogues, not realizing that they do not listen to his words but instead only want some of his actions.

The lack of wholeness in the other characters corresponds to Aron's own sense of fragmentation: they seem to represent dichotomies within him rather than independent characters. Agnes and Lilly stand for the dichotomy between love and lust, Evangeline for that between love and work, Berglund, between love and society, and Brinkman for the dichotomy between love and power.

Love here defines spiritual life; the other components represent principles of this world. The body embraces spirit *and* world together, but its unity of form is divided into two kinds of consciousness: natural and intellectual. Natural consciousness is uncorrupted by societal considerations. We find this sentiment illustrated in the scene with Aron scratching the murderer, who in his sleep is only a person with a body, not a criminal. Intellectual consciousness belongs to culture with its limitations and evaluations.

Naturally the two types of consciousness cannot replace each other or invalidate each other because they belong to different realms of existence. But Aron does not understand this. Therefore he is trying the impossible, Nielsen argues: "to revoke consciousness

with consciousness." He does not understand his body[40] and consequently does not understand nature. He acts contrary to his own intentions when he tries to please everyone, and in so doing we may
claim that he imposes his will upon affairs of the spirit. His actions
become, to use an existentialist expression, inauthentic, because they
are basically insincere and ultimately inconsequential to his own
fate. "His will," Nielsen continues, explaining the nature of Aron's
piety, "has not yielded to the insight that there are things you cannot will."[41] You cannot, for example, will to save everyone from their
miseries.

This Dora tries to tell Aron during one of his absurd performances
as Savior in the forest with Agnes and Lilly. Dora, Aron's foil, accepts the limitations of this world without excluding the infinity of
God's. She embraces simultaneously her profane identity as political
worker and her spiritual identity as a Christian by hiding her Christian identity from her worldly allegiances. The world sees only Dora,
the cleaning woman and socialist, and knows nothing about her
spiritual existence. She is one of Ahlin's many Kierkegaardian
characters, persons who, like Kierkegaard's tax collector, disguise
their Christian nature under a pedestrian or "lowly" social image.

Aron does not heed Dora, however, and becomes more and more
distracted from his original intentions. Not even when he discovers
that his briefcase with the tombstone is gone does he revoke his
promise to follow Brinkman, so that instead he may find his stone
and complete his mission. He is totally subjected to Brinkman, the
character of will, whom he follows in his search for order. When
Brinkman dies, so dies Aron's last attempt to restore order in his existence. Aron, who has been all too eager to act, becomes passive,
loses his will without gaining sense; everything becomes more bizarre and nonsensical.

When Brinkman falls into the river, Aron runs, he thinks, in the
same direction as the river runs. But he does not run; he thinks:

I have experienced how I will arrive at the place where I stand tied and half
dead. Love makes alive. See, I stand up. The spirit leaves the body. For you
[Divine Eros] transform yourself downward so that we may transform
ourself upward. How would we be able to transform downward? Here we
are already down. Can a prisoner capture himself? (277)

Here he interprets God's love in platonic-logical terms instead of
Christian-irrational terms, which indicates his definite dependence
on a system of thought based upon societal concepts or intellectual

consciousness. This constitutes his ultimate failure. And shortly thereafter he himself dies, tied to his past, unliberated, his mission unaccomplished. His body never rises again, for he never replaced intellectual with natural consciousness, and his body remains corrupted by his will and social lusts. Like Evangeline, he failed to place himself outside an intellectual frame of reference which could enable him to raise spirit *and* body through God's grace. Finishing his temporal life in this mood, he dies a death without grace.

IV   Cinnamon Girl

A   *The plot: Growing consciousness of life's dichotomies*

Britt-Marie, called Cinnamon Girl[42] by her mother Sylvia, is a thirteen-year-old of unusual freedom and maturity. She seems at times more like the mother of her mother, a beautiful factory worker with a talent for enjoying life intensely, particularly when she is in love.

Her mother has a new lover. She is not yet comfortable enough to bring her daughter and her lover together, so Britt-Marie will stay away the night he comes for dinner for the first time. As a bribe, Britt-Marie had asked for a toy ocarina. Playing and dancing in the sunset, she pretends to be her own brother and sister. Then she sneaks into an outdoor restaurant and meets a young man, Arnold.

She tells him her ideas about God and man, and how they each belong to their sphere, man to earth and God to water: "... when you walk on water, you fall into the depth right into God" (77). The adults, she believes, walk on the earth, free and happy, because that is their proper locus as human beings; she still walks on water, however, because she has not found her locus. When the adults become old and helpless they will again walk on water, but then they are ready to fall into God. To be ready for this fall man must first come of age, she explains, man must love and live in happiness in this world. Then God's love will take man to His world to live in bliss. Arnold, already trapped in a man-made value system, does not understand why man cannot immediately join the best world:

— I don't want to be imprisoned in the hell of the adjectives.
I don't want to crawl around in the dungeons of the words of qualities. . . .
Qualities cannot discriminate conclusively between people. . . . Our loneliness is no quality. It is a position. . . . To be alone is to be in your own locus. And as long as we exist we must always exist in a locus. No one can save us alive from our locus.

— He who loses his life will win it.
— Who says so?
— Love. You have never loved. Therefore you have no faith. (78 - 79)

Then she kisses him and he runs away.

As her mother's love affair continues, Britt-Marie becomes increasingly wary of its effect on her mother, who moves jerkily and awkwardly in her room as if she did not belong there. Sylvia battles with her passion for the lover and her contempt for his wife, who holds on to him by her extreme willingness to forgive his escapades. Britt-Marie stays away from her mother because the energy she develops in her battle threatens to burn her.

Left to herself, she spends most of her time with a little old woman in a button and sewing store who teaches her to embroider. The woman, soon destined to die, tells Britt-Marie about the futility of striving for perfection in life, and about the glory of work and service, however trivial. Not daring to undertake the commitment of love, she had lived "undeveloped" and in despair until a day when she realized that the significance of being a physical being meant to have a body which could give her the joy of work. Shortly after talking to the woman, Britt-Marie learns that her dog friend has been killed. She rescues his body from a garbage can and buries him ceremoniously in a glade.

The woman's story and the dog's death make Britt-Marie aware that the body is necessary for peace of mind, but that at the same time it does not indicate the nature of mind. Therefore the filthy dog carcass cannot destroy her fundamental notion of the dog as a beautiful being. While she is still in this serene mood, her mother appears, physically deteriorated, beaten, and mentally deranged. Her lover has left her, politely thanking her for a nice time (and asking her to clean up the place before she leaves). Sylvia's despair, her sense of having been used and found useless, is so profound that she can only articulate her feelings by inarticulate screaming, culminating in her blaming Britt-Marie for having destroyed her joy of life by moralism.

Unable to comfort her, Britt-Marie leaves and walks out into the night where she meets Arnold and follows him to his room. She feels nonexistent and unreal; she needs to be assured of her existence. In the semidarkness of his room filled with music, "experience in ordered form," they undress and engage in a ritual of love performed in the meeting of their eyes. As in the love scene between Aron and Evangeline in *Pious Murders*, the ecstacy of love is created by their eyes; their bodies seem only as a temple, to hold their eyes.

Back home she finds her mother still trapped in her suffering, wordless, her body passively in bed. Then Sylvia collects herself and decides to get her lover back on any terms. Britt-Marie listens helplessly to her mother's calculations and manipulations. Sylvia's insistence on twisting life to fit her desires for immediate gratification of lust arouses in Britt-Marie the wish that she might be possessed by the wrath of love capable of annihilating the degrading qualities within her mother:[43] "Oh, why are we not taught the right wrath? . . . She saw how necessary wrath is. There was much she ought to destroy. But where were the right limits? How was she to separate that which must go from that which must remain?" (185). Without this wrath she cannot save her mother, who orders her to meet Stellan when he returns from his wife and tell him that Sylvia loves him.

Britt-Marie meets Stellan but she tells him Sylvia never wants to see him again. Realizing that her lies had been mere illusions of wrath and that she has deceived herself, she must make penance. Therefore she sacrifices a box of small objects she has taken from adults whom she had loved and admired. She is now herself old. She has known the sacred element of love through Arnold and has seen lust rage in her mother. Helpless in spite of her insights, she feels she has experienced more than enough and wishes for peace in death.

First she will try to free her mother's lover from his wife, Hildur. She implies to Hildur that Stellan has been indecent with her, a mere child, and that she now loves him with tormenting intensity. Hildur listens disgusted but fascinated as Britt-Marie speaks about her love with a fervor echoing her mother's passion and despair. Britt-Marie seems to blend the identities not only between herself and her mother, but also between her own lover and her mother's lover. Her world has lost order and sense. She walks up to the top of a hill and climbs on to a shelf where she lies down and begins to sing.

Calling for "Cinnamon Girl," Sylvia and her lover follow the traces of paper ribbons Britt-Marie has left behind. Reaching the peak of the hill they look into each other's eyes "and the world around them united and stood in singular meaning," an experience of love resembling Britt-Marie's and Arnold's earlier. As they approach the place where Cinnamon Girl lies, they hear a song like none they have heard before:

She sang but the melody did not seem to want to harmonize. At the same time she was making gestures with her uplifted hands. They saw what she did with her hands. She tried to combine them to different figures but somehow it did not work. (234)

They saw the girl lift her arms. She seemed to want to make them form a wreath around her head, but it did not seem to succeed. Her arms fell down. . . . Now the girl turned around and took two small steps. Then she took a longer step straight out into the air. (235)

B *Failure in life, victory in death*

Britt-Marie suffers from her transient identity, as Örjan Lindberger says, from being "a half-person (*halvvarelse*) who is neither child nor adult, neither true nor false."[44] She is also torn between moral dislike for her mother's life and love for her nevertheless. She hates her condition and dreams about growing up, about becoming an adult because, as she says, "They can love. That is paradise on earth. I hate. I want to destroy myself. But how will I then reach Paradise?" (144). Her hatred of self is old, born when she as a little girl understood that her very existence prevented her mother from enjoying life.

She is still formless and Ahlin's technique of expressing his characters' psychological state through their physical movements or, like Dostoevski, Faulkner, and Sartre, in ritual, is in the character of Britt-Marie expressed beautifully with her hands. "Her hands become," Allan Fagerström observes, "the silent expression of the ecstatic ritual of growing. Her hands accompany every silent experience of the adult world; the already formed world. They round off every meeting with the adult existence, which with all its realism has no more tangible criterion than Cinnamon Girl's own alienation."[45] Britt-Marie's confusion is particularly acute when Sylvia has declared firmly that she will not return to her lover until he leaves his wife and yet allows him to talk her into continuing their relationship. She listens to the discussion:

Britt-Marie tried to understand what she heard. She worked with her hands to bring forth a resemblance. She did not succeed. Her hands were too cool and too delicately built. They could not create caricatures. They could create the forms of pain, evil, and wrath. But not this, not these abstractly hot, abstractly furry, abstractly intimate, and abstractly inimical voices. (110)

But later when Sylvia has been arrogantly dismissed by Stellan and comes home suffering and blaming Britt-Marie for her miseries, Britt-Marie is again able to retain her sense of form. Suffering, evil, and wrath, she understands: "In her head she still knew what is important and desirable in this life, and when she lifted her hands she was still able to create forms she knew were beautiful" (165). She lacks, however, a feeling of substance:

She could play, but where was the safe reality one needs to play with, and on, and against? She did not transform the serious and the simple to a game. She was the empty transformation itself. She was nothing. . . . She created nothingnesses in the empty air from nonexisting matter. (167)

Overwhelmed by her loneliness and isolation, she ultimately decides that she loves her mother and must help her, though she recognizes her mother's inability to differentiate between truths and lies, her inclination to manipulate reality and change "the past, the present and her self" (171). Shortly after this insight she follows Arnold to his room and through their ritualistic performance of an act of love she obtains form. Projecting herself into the future, she envisions Arnold as her husband and in their love she has found an identity: she has become a person.

This identity is, however, only a vision of the future; her present love, her mother, does not love her. Her identity is therefore still ambiguous, a "between" form which simultaneously exists and does not exist. When Sylvia commands her to act as an intercessor to bring Stellan back to her, Britt-Marie breaks her promise to do so, because she is confused about the nature of her true self. Seeking to define herself she whispers her own name, but this does not bring her closer to herself. Then she invents a sequence of lies intended to save her mother from further indignities in her relationship with Stellan. She wants to force her mother to live a worthier life, but she soon realizes that the result of these attempts is a desecration of her own true self. She cannot guide Sylvia's life in the right direction and make her live up to an image of adult perfection and ideal. And, Britt-Marie understands, it has also been impossible for herself to remain pure and above unworthy acts.

Her death, then, as Gunnar Brandell points out, is a result of her failure to accomplish total perfection.[46] She lived a sinner, for she did indeed sin in her pursuit of perfection, which (as Luther repeatedly argues) is impossible to achieve. Only God can be perfect. By pursuing perfection man will ultimately find that the laws he employs to measure his results and reach his goals become ends in themselves. Man thus risks death from the laws of his own creation. She dies a saint, however, for her fall "turns into an upward curve where it touches the ground" because she falls, like her father, for love, into God's love: "Her love was infinite. . . . She would sacrifice herself. Her whole life. . . . As soon as she heard her name called she would stand up: Cinnamon Girl, Cinnamon Girl. She would crumble herself so that the calling mouth might taste the sweetness of life" (16). So she says to herself in the beginning of the novel, having just caught a last glimpse of her mother going to work. At the end her predictions are fulfilled: As Sylvia and Stellan walk up the hill calling "Cinnamon Girl," she stands up and steps out into space, thus giving life to Sylvia while losing her own. By this act, her failure in life is transformed into a victory in death.

CHAPTER 4

Failure of Values

WHEN man makes his sense of dignity dependent upon how he conforms to standards and norms established outside himself (for social convenience and purpose), he inevitably sees himself as a failure when his individual situation appears inferior to the ideals of a collective standard. He cannot change the social ideals by himself, only his own attitudes toward them. But he can decide to what extent he will allow society to define his individual worth.

To come to such a decision he must undergo a change of consciousness, either through a form of death as discussed earlier, or through compromise with the ideals. The works to be discussed in the latter context are the three novels immediately following *My Death Is My Own: Om (If, About, Around,* 1946), *Jungfrun i det gröna (Nigella Damascena,* 1947) and *Egen spis (A Stove of One's Own,* 1948). Of the three novels, *If, About, Around* is the most important. It is Ahlin's most innovative and daring experiment with narrative structure and a most thorough account of the destructiveness of social standards.

I If, About, Around

A *The plot: The abandoned son*

Sixteen-year-old Bengt and his father Peter have been thrown out by Matilda, one of the many women who have been taking care of them over the years. Peter's only ambition is to find a woman who will provide him with security for the rest of his life and he spares no effort to reach his goal. One of his more effective means has been to appeal to women's maternal instincts by presenting Bengt as a poor, motherless child desperately needing maternal care. To make Bengt more amenable to the different mother figures passing through his life, Peter has been pretending that each new woman is indeed

Bengt's real mother, while the previous "real" mother was a mistake or a lie.

Over the years, however, Bengt's demand to know the truth has grown stronger and Peter has been forced to add a new "real" each time they have moved: this is your "real mother," "real, real mother," "absolutely real mother," etc. Bengt is now tired of all the mothers and wants his father and himself to become self-supporting and independent. Even though Peter has been a poor father, often lied to Bengt, stolen his money, and used him for his own selfish purposes, Bengt loves him.

Peter pretends to agree with Bengt about an independent life, but in fact keeps an eye open for another opportunity to avoid responsibility, by catching another woman. For temporary shelter they go to the river hoping to find an old cargo boat, and on their way they collect empty bottles to sell for cash. They also meet some old friends and make new ones.

First they meet a woman called "Stockholmsbåten" ("The Stockholm Boat"). Her highest desire in life is to be regarded as a lady from Stockholm, and she is willing to do anything to convey such an impression. Bengt makes a fool of her to demonstrate the shallowness of her ideals.

Next they meet Oscar sleeping drunk on a couple of boards. He is waiting for his sister, Sofia, to take him home. Oscar talks to Bengt about Peter and Sofia in terms which make Bengt suspect that Sofia is his true mother. Before he can confirm his suspicions, Sofia appears and prevents Oscar from revealing the truth. The whole time they are together she turns her back to Bengt, as a symbol of her rejection of Bengt and her motherhood. Peter soon returns with a handcart and while Oscar is being wheeled home, he carries on a long discourse about the myth of motherhood, Western culture, and the father figure as symbols of social order and structure.

After the encounter with Oscar and Sofia, Bengt and Peter find a boat to sleep in. There they are joined by a man, Spinnet, waiting for his wife to return with her lover from a trip in Spinnet's boat. Though he is upset about his wife having a lover, he pretends that he is really only concerned about her having brought his best fishing rod along. He tells Peter that when she returns, he is going to show who is the master of the house. But when she does return with her lover, he loses his strong-willed attitude and impotently watches them unload the boat and disappear together. He settles with Peter and Bengt for the night and Bengt tells a story about the masochistic perch, Masso, who ate his own eye three times to please a fisherwoman he loved. Then Peter gives Spinnet advice on how to handle his wife and borrows money from him.

The next day Bengt and Peter are awakened as they are hit by another boat. The other boat is a tug boat owned by the independent and able widow, Herkula, who runs it with the help of her brother-in-law, Långlatus. As soon as Peter realizes who they are, he sees his big chance: if he could catch Herkula, he would live comfortably for the rest of his life. Bengt immediately understands that his own plans for an independent life with Peter are jeopardized by Herkula's appearance. Therefore he makes Peter promise to let his designs concerning Herkula wait for a day, while Bengt pursues his secret plan to get them the money that will make them independent. They agree to meet again at a certain time and place. However, Peter never intends to keep his promise, and while Bengt is gone he manages to get on board Herkula's boat.

In the meantime, Bengt is visiting Henrik Fager, a man completely dominated by his widowed mother. He cannot get a woman by himself and he wants Bengt and Peter to furnish him with suitable sex objects, a service for which he will pay them well. Bengt envisions a carefree future for himself and Peter with all the money they can get from this business, and makes a deal with Henrik. Then he returns to meet Peter, who does not come.

Waiting for Peter, Bengt lets his imagination play with the events which could have occurred. He understands that Peter has not kept his promise, and he now envisions the course of Peter's courtship with Herkula. He imagines that Herkula has set as a condition for allowing Peter to live with her that he buy her a car. Though Peter has no idea where he would get the money he agrees to do so and in this opportune moment Sofia reappears wanting to give Peter Bengt's maternal inheritance, provided Peter gives Bengt an education. This Peter promises, but instead keeps the money himself and leaves Bengt after having accused the boy of destroying his life.

This vision makes Bengt desperately unhappy. Soon he meets an old man, Peter Sjökvist, whom he wants to make into a substitute father to care for as he has cared for Peter. Peter Sjökvist, however, having been rejected himself all his life, does not understand that Bengt wants him. In a grotesque sequence of events he too abandons Bengt; he dies.

The novel ends with an epilogue in which Ahlin presents various possibilities for Bengt's future.

B *Point of view*

With Bengt as focal point, the point of view changes frequently between an impersonal narrator, a first person narrator, and Bengt, who is at times identical to the narrator, and at other times observed by the impersonal narrator. In some sections the reader is addressed in second person by the narrator; in other passages the implied author addresses Bengt. There are also philosophical discussions and editorial comments by the implied author. Each type of narrator intrudes upon the others' narrative, thus creating a complex interchange of narrative perspectives.

We find, for example, paragraphs beginning with Bengt seen in third person by an impersonal narrator, and ending with his thoughts articulated in second person by the narrator: "Bengt saw that something happened to Peter's feelings at that moment, something difficult, something that can be compared only to blood suddenly squirting from a body. And I who cannot apply a dressing you felt, what's going to happen now?" (80).[1] Or, there are passages beginning in the second person and ending in third person: "A crazy suspicion seized you. It is she, you thought. . . . Sofia is my real mother, my absolutely real mother . . . Bengt thought" (151). Or, we find a third person narrator interrupted by Bengt as the first person narrator: "Then Långlatus tried to pull his hand back but now his hand's movement was tough like hard rubber. . . . His hand flew away to its duty and so he did this and that and how do I know how one starts a tug boat" (290). We may also find Bengt first as a character seen by an impersonal narrator, then as narrator/character speaking about his father, finally shifting into narrator/character addressing his father: all in one paragraph:

But it was not so that Bengt now went hoping that after this the feelings of my old man and myself will meet more often, for from now on I can look higher up without him saying "keep out of this." How we walk together again and we will continue that so at the end you will walk the way I want you to. . . . (17)

By this technique the reader must constantly reorient himself in relation to the characters, and his "willing suspension of disbelief" does not last very long, if it has ever developed.

C *Illusion*

If, About, Around constitutes Ahlin's most consistently constructed alternative to, and reaction against, the "novel of illusion," which he calls works written in the tradition of Flaubertian realism. He discusses his aesthetics in the novel itself in a chapter called "The White Hunger of the Lie." Here he explains that the traditional form of the novel can hardly be justified in today's society which lacks the cohesiveness, morally, politically, economically, and socially, of the society which provided the "rear-screen projected" background for the novel of illusion.

. . . these sentences are not intended to convey the illusion of "organic life." They are meant to throb in a blood vessel of associations generated by you as a reader. . . .

It might happen that your associations are guided by demands for naturalism or tastes, unknown to me. The word situation as it has been developed in these pages has maybe not at all inspired you, hypnotized you, or appealed to you so that you, softly yielding, associate the way I intended you to. The mere fact that I suddenly begin to talk to you maybe annoys you. . . .

But if it does, I have then succeeded in creating a relationship between the word situation in these pages and your system of associations. (329)

My words throbbing in your system of associations is my model, my working material, my intention. This book is not about Bengt, not about Peter, not about Herkula or any one else, but about you. (330)

The implied author also makes the reader aware of the written character of the novel by analyzing the text: "You and me, one went on thinking. Oh, you and me! Behind this 'you,' Peter is obviously hidden, while we behind 'me' naturally find Bengt himself. 'And' ties them together in an 'and-ish' way and the interjection 'oh' illustrates excellently the emotional charge then present in Bengt's soul-breast-heart, etc" (99). Instead of Flaubert's form of realism, Ahlin prefers the tradition which we trace from romantic irony, via Thackeray, to the French and German novel of the 1920s, to André Gide and Thomas Mann, both documented sources of inspiration for Ahlin.

D The multisubject

To emphasize the fact that the novel is intended to appeal to each reader insofar as he provides the "rear-screen projected" background himself, Ahlin leaves out all descriptions of setting which are not absolutely necessary to provide a character with a place to sit or walk, and even in those instances, he gives no more than rudimentary information. Furthermore, Ahlin invents a "multisubject" containing first, second, and third person, thereby

stressing the universality of his protagonist Bengt, and simultaneously depriving him of individuality from a realistic point of view.
Bengt is not a person, as much as a personification of an idea: "Life
is hell! thought *Bengt who is you who are I*. And then they demand
that we behave ourselves or write novels just like anybody else" (53)
(Italics mine). The multisubject may vary slightly in its order of
persons, but it always contains all three persons. By the "we," Ahlin
here makes the reader, the "you," cocreator of the novel. It is
Ahlin's contention that an intellectual dialogue between reader and
writer should replace emotional identification between reader and
character which the Flaubertian type of novel encourages.[2] He establishes an intellectual intercourse by disturbing his reader's conventional expectations of continuity of form. The "multisubject,"
both by its length and its diversified point of view, insures against
any nonreflective reading. So does the fact that, as gleaned from the
above examples, there is, in general, no absolute point of reference
regarding the identity of personal pronouns throughout the novel.

E *Characterization*
  This does not mean that the writer himself is totally unbiased or
detached from his text and his characters. The novel is, after all,
about Bengt, whose thoughts as well as actions are recorded in
greater detail than those of other characters:

Note! As the reader has maybe already noticed that the writer who is you
who are Bengt who is our unknown contemporary friend, does not identify
as closely with Peter. That is why we only occasionally have informed about
what Peter feels and thinks. We keep more to his actions, looking at him
from outside. (101)

This may give the impression that the writer is using a traditional
omniscient point of view at least as far as Bengt is concerned. The
nature and language of Bengt's thoughts are, however, not conventionally realistic. He is too young and too uneducated for the ideas
ascribed to him or the form in which they are articulated.
  Ulf Linde even sees him as "a structure of words first becoming
alive when we mirror ourselves in them."[3] That is, each reader
creates his own image of Bengt, depending upon the associations
which the "Bengt-elements" in the novel awaken within him.
Bengt, in other words, may not evoke identical images in different
readers. However, this does not make him unreal in the sense of being unbelievable; he is merely unique.

Spinnet and Peter, on the other hand, are definitely acting beyond any credible frame of reference in the dialogue following the ritual Spinnet has performed in removing his wallet from a buttoned-up pocket inside his jacket. Peter watches him, fascinated, and asks whether or not Spinnet's mother had been married. Spinnet confesses she was not, whereupon Peter points at the pocket with the wallet:

— Wrong! cried-said-whispered Peter for Bengt was not to be awakened and in fact there are many leading verbs in the Swedish language. It's wrong all of it! Take what I now say symbolically but as a one hundred percent accurate symbol. *That is a hymen.*
Peter scratched again at the sewed-on flap.
— A hymen? Spinnet whispered and understood that he must constantly encounter incomprehensible things.
— Your mother's, Peter added, though he had not read a word of psychoanalysis.
— Are you stupid or. . .
— It is hers, the one she gave up but which she sewed on to you from within and outside, in heart and on clothes so that you would not come into her situation. She sewed a lot of hymens on to you so that you would always have one left if you were to fall and let someone take any of them.
— You're crazy, said Spinnet but felt that Peter probably was on the side of reality, though he had not read anything about psychoanalysis either. (207)

Spinnet and Peter are here given insights they admittedly could not possess. The author treats his characters as marionettes, but they are not marionettes in the Thackerayan sense or like the characters in the novels of Hjalmar Bergman, whose characters/marionettes acted consistently within their own given frame of reference; that is not so with Ahlin's character here. They illustrate the contention that Ahlin's characters are word constructs and follow other rules of behavior than the reader would expect, thus contributing to a sense of detachment between reader and character.

He creates hereby an ironic distance similar to the one created by Kierkegaard's many pseudonyms in *Either-Or.* They are characters in name only, creations of the writer's brain, though superficially they seem to possess separate identities.

F   *Words*

Word structure also contributes to keeping the reader aware that the novel is a construction of words, not a slice of life. This effect is obtained in particular through the use of several words-for-one strung together by hyphens:

Bengt took one step forward and looked down on her. To describe what he then felt-perceived-experienced we cannot be satisfied with a description of his emotions. . . . (109)

My mouth does its best. I cannot keep it in a definite position. The pain-bitterness-joy-despair-pleasure pushes it now here now there. (31)

Lies! Peter Sjökvist shouted at Bengt. In the back room (*lillkammaren*) I have only locked up all fallen walls, everything I could have had for my sons' achievement-purpose-result. (358)

The method gives the reader an opportunity to become actively in-volved in the creative process, since he will probably be inclined to emphasize one of the words above the other, according to his per-sonal understanding of the situation. Or, he may shift with each word into a new perception of the situation. Either way he must stop to think about the words and cannot read along spellbound by them. Ahlin has thus created a form of reader participation in the work, more immediate than the traditional methods of including the reader in an authorial "we" or addressing him with "you."

Other methods of reminding the reader of his reading activity are the use of names and the play on word meaning. The first chapter, as Erik A. Nielsen observes, uses names of streetcar stops to highlight events from Peter's and Bengt's lives in a way parodying the in-troductory chapter of the traditional novel, in which characters are presented and background information given.[4] Matilda has thrown Peter out after a fight and consequently the first stop is called "Quarrel Alley." Another stop exposing Peter's character is named "Trick Street." Peter's winding justification for begging Matilda to take him back occurs at the stop "Zig-Zag Path."

In the following chapter, Ahlin plays upon the fact that in Swedish, certain verbs in the present tense and certain nouns in the plural are spelled the same way. The scene begins with Bengt trying to prevent Peter from returning to Matilda, and Peter does not know what to do about his unexpected change in life: "He acted in other words exactly as if he were lying in the water and then yelled to his friends on the rocks: — Hi there. Do you see me? Look, for now I'll try to reach the bottom here" (67). The scene dramatizes Peter's psy-chological state of mind. He is in unknown waters and does not know where he can find stability: a new woman. Bengt tries to make him forget women by offering him a beer and goads him toward a bar: "— Peg along [run] Dad. We'll make it as long as you peg along [run]" (68). The verb "peg" (*pinnar*) transfers into a noun in the

sentence immediately following: "you can make a raftfrom pegs
(*pinnar*) . . ." which then forms the transition to the original image
of Peter in the water: "If the old man stays in the water too long he
may get cramps or chills or perhaps a heart attack. For it cannot be
good for your heart to keep reaching for the bottom continuously,
that is: trying to reach for the bottom unsuccessfully" (68). This Joycean playing with metaphors and grammar leads one away from any
implied nineteenth-century sentimentality in the story: a son trying
to save his father from an unworthy existence. The potential
emotional involvement with Bengt's problem becomes instead an intellectual appreciation of Ahlin's verbal wit. He creates a comical effect when running (pegging along) turns into an imagined raft to
rescue a man mentally in the deep water. Here ironic distance is
mixed with humorous compassion in a way typical of Ahlin.

G   Man degraded by values

If, About, Around, Ulf Linde says, is a polemic against modern
man's dependence upon cultural values and social norms as bases for
his sense of security.[5] Such values are meaningless as guidelines
because they, like Bengt's mothers, are defined in terms of assumed
and therefore replaceable characteristics. They are not absolute and
constant. Peter, however, needs them so that he can avoid taking
any responsibility himself for his life. He seeks a woman who wants
to serve as Bengt's mother, not for Bengt's sake, but for his own: the
woman's ultimate function is to provide Peter with a life of comfort
and security, to be his "fat pension."

Despite constant failures, he continues to pretend that his most recent woman is the "real" mother. He does not perceive the absurdity of adding on "real's," as if motherhood were a rank which
secured legitimacy by sheer force of comparison for the highest
placed person. In the process he loses his dignity and integrity
because he will lie and cheat if it serves his purpose. He knows that
he pursues mere illusions, since the only true mother figure, Sofia,
has rejected both him and Bengt, and yet he prefers the illusion of
security to having to rely on his own resources.

Bengt, on the other hand, wants to liberate Peter from his
dependence on such false ideals. He, like Britt-Marie in *Cinnamon
Girl,* wants to take care of his parent, and save him from an unworthy existence. Bengt wants to be his "father's father" (45), which
means, Nielsen explains, that "he must himself accomplish what his
father never had the strength of character or patience to do. He

wants to create a bourgeois frame for their lives, to give his father a respectable social position and make him a better being."[6] Bengt's problem is identical to Britt-Marie's, and the two children also resemble each other in the sense that they are more mature than their parents and love them in spite of the latters' shortcomings which sometimes make them suffer.

Not even Bengt's declaration that he loves Peter can make Peter give up his need to confirm his value through being accepted by a system, represented by the women-mothers. One person's love is not enough to balance the weight of a whole established value system. Instead, Bengt's love, ironically, makes Peter believe that he is, after all, not bad: "No, I cannot be such a bastard, Peter maintained and felt that he had reached bottom in himself and was standing in his own reality. The boy is standing there as a living proof, he thought . . ." (91). Love must be deserved according to Peter's logic and so he turns Bengt's love for him into an excuse for refusing to see the truth about himself and for not changing his life.

The reader, however, sees the shallowness of Peter's concept of self and his ideals. This attitude is further exposed in other characters' weakness for decorating themselves with borrowed importance and value. One of these characters is "Stockholmsbåten" ("The Stockholm Boat") who illustrates the lack of dignity resulting from identifying one's self in terms alien to that self.

"The Stockholm Boat" does not question Bengt's information about what defines a lady from Stockholm. She is oblivious to the comic apparition she offers, dressed in what she believes to be proper Stockholmian fashion: rolled down stockings, a skirt unbottoned over her hips and a brown paper bag for a hat. She, like Peter, would rather be undignified than left without the security gained from feeling comfortably settled in her chosen role.

The episode with "Stockholmsbåten," Linde explains, lets "Bengt witness the degradation resulting from belief in a 'truth' as it is perceived by someone standing outside of it. A real lady from Stockholm," Linde points out, "would have made the whole scene impossible. But Stockholm ladies are in Stockholm, which means that the truth is not with us,"[7] but elsewhere, we might add, outside our realm of experience. "Stockholmsbåten" herself does not realize that she is a victim of her own illusions about reality.

Spinnet, the cuckold husband who puts his foot down when his wife is out of reach and keeps his mouth shut when she appears, is another example of a person who escapes the truth about himself through manipulations. In his case the manipulations deal with concrete things, unlike "Stockholmsbåten's" facts. He surrounds his pipe smoking with rituals as if he were performing a sacred act, and talks about his fishing rod as if it were a loved woman. In fact, he is manipulating his things to mask his despair and feelings of inferiority.

Linde draws a parallel between Spinnet's preoccupation with things as a manifestation of security, and the church's preserving "her dogmas through decorations and cathedrals," or "the materialistic belief in science as consolidated in cars, televisions, and other products for consumption. . . ."[8] Just as things cannot save man from despair, neither can man be saved by man-made credos such as Communism, discussed in *Tåbb with the Manifesto*, or psychoanalysis, or any "isms."

Henrik Fager, cradled in the comfort provided by his mother's engulfing care, is another example of an existence demeaned by its value system. He has lost all power of action by accepting the norm his mother has provided for his life. From time to time he has, however, been bothered by dreams of a graceful and pretty little woman, very different from his mother. His dream woman does not possess property and wealth, and in this respect she does not conform to the ideal his father had set up for him. Only lately can he merge the different ideals, his own and his father's, into one image: "He enjoyed the sight of a fine-limbed girl enthroned on top of the town's biggest house, stretched out like on a lush couch. Then Henrik was quite drunk. He was happy too, for in his dream his conditioned ideals and his physical personal desire had merged in a blessed union. He felt peace in his heart, harmony in his life" (275). But his ideal is a dream image only, in reality he cannot get any woman by himself, but must employ Bengt and Peter for this purpose.

H *Collapse of values*

Oscar, the schoolteacher, learned but dilapidated, functions in *If, About, Around* much like Staffan Hyrell in *Tåbb with the Manifesto,* namely as a spokesman for the author and a truth-sayer to the protagonist. Ironically, Oscar, during his discourse on the impotence and meaninglessness of societal and cultural norms, is himself drunk to immobility, lying on a handcart pulled by Peter and Sofia, who represent the very principles he is deriding: the father and the mother.

He sets modern man's problem, and consequently also Bengt's, in relation to his cultural conditioning in terms resembling the thoughts of the Grand Inquisitor in *The Brothers Karamazov*, a work Oscar also refers to in his discourse on man's dependence on the father culture manifested in past achievements and inherited values. The Grand Inquisitor, explicating the Devil's challenging Christ in the desert to turn stones into bread, says:

Choosing "bread," Thou wouldst have satisfied the universal and everlasting craving of humanity — to find someone to worship. . . . But man seeks to worship what is established beyond dispute, so that all men would agree at once to worship. . . . This craving for *community* of worship is the chief misery of every man individually and of all humanity from the beginning of time.[9]

The work of the father provided the "community of worship" in the form of social structure, culture, economic, and political order. All of these the son constantly crushed in revolutions and reforms, Oscar points out, only "to establish himself as father" (155), not to eliminate the principle itself.

Bengt, though he wants to govern his own life, is not independent of the father principle: he does not want to abandon or reject Peter, only to change him and make him adopt Bengt's own values. Instead of a liberated mind, Bengt demonstrates in his desire to reform his father an ironic dependence on the very values he wants to change. "The father should not prevent us from becoming independent persons" (152), Oscar preaches, and advises Bengt to live his own free life because Peter is worthless and unreliable. But Bengt refuses to accept Oscar's judgment of Peter and besides, he has already declared that he loves Peter regardless of his lack of merit. His love for Peter is, however, not totally unselfish; it rests partly on his fear of being left to his own resources: ". . . I must be able to restore my father from his decadence; I must succeed or else nothing will succeed for me" (157). Bengt does not yet realize that he is tied to Peter not by love but by the system he wants Peter to disown.

However, confronted by Henrik Fager and his mother, Bengt understands that his concern for Peter has an ultimately stifling effect on his own development. Mrs. Fager "understands" Henrik to the extent that she does not give him any free living space in which he can grow into an independent person. Passively, Henrik accepts his mother's smothering care and resembles a fat overgrown baby more than an adult man. The situation, a reversal of the relationship between Bengt and Peter, shows Bengt in a grotesque manner, the absurdity of his attempts to form Peter after his own ideals. Yet he insists on wanting to change Peter, because of his impossible wish to "eliminate something which is simply a condition of life."[10] But no matter how much Peter degrades himself, thus making Bengt suffer, Bengt will never be able to change the basic condition of his life, namely that Peter is his father and must be accepted as he is.

Though Bengt needs some form of father principle in his life, he is less dependent on the mother principle, which, Oscar explains, is manifest in the myth about personal providence personified in mother nature and a mother church, those providers of earthly and spiritual life. The myth disintegrated when the mother saw herself as an individual "I," which, Oscar continues, happened in Ibsen's *A Doll House*. There Nora, who is the liberated woman of the Western world, "forced by liberalism and with the help of Ibsen, experienced herself as an independent person" (149).

When the mother idea, nature and the church, was deprived of its superiority over man by science and the Reformation, only an "I" was left, an "I" who felt it existed because of its doubts, but the giving, protecting superior "mother-you" was dead: "All personalized guarantors of our existence had ceased to exist. Consequently, all norms of value must lose their so-called objective foundation, for only a You can create that. . . . We are standing alone in our I and must create our own values" (152). This is exactly what Bengt wants and therefore he is disturbed by the thought that he might, after all, have a mother. Bengt's suspicion about Sofia's true identity grows as Oscar's parallels between Sofia and Nora become more explicit. "Sofia is my real mother, my absolutely real, real mother! She abandoned Peter because she did not think he was worth much and me because she realized she would not be able to make a man out of me the way she was" (151). The mother figure denounces her husband for his lack of worth and abandons the son for her own lack of substance, thus leaving him in an emotional vacuum expressed here, as so often in Ahlin's work, in terms of a physical sensation: "Then he did not feel he was walking" (151). Bengt tries to fill the empty space in his existence with his unconditional love for Peter, but fails because he translates his emotional needs into dreams about social survival independent of mother figures: work rather than worship will be his manifestations of love.

Tired of Bengt's interferences with his life, particularly with his attempts to keep him from Herkula, Peter finally screams at him: "You have destroyed my life . . . you have spoiled the pitiful rest of life that is left in me" (345). The same parental rebellion against the moralism of their children is also echoed by Britt-Marie's mother in *Cinnamon Girl*.

Gradually Bengt realizes that he cannot be his "father's father":

You cannot reverse the order. A father must himself live up to the demands of fatherhood. No one can do it for him. If he cannot fulfill the strict demands he is a failure and will always feel like a failure as long as the demands remain within him. His whole life will be filled by attempts to escape to a place where the demands cease to be valid. He reaches for soothing remedies, for manipulations and dialectics, for new consciences and other experiences. (346)

Nor does he feel competent to be a father's son, and in this situation of temporary confusion about his identity he meets the old man Peter Sjökvist, a man in need of a son. Bengt decides to live with him and become his son, but Peter Sjökvist has been too often cheated by life to be able to accept Bengt as his son and dies instead, hugging a rag doll and surrounded by doll beds he had made during his long but empty life. The beds symbolize his wish for children, continuation of life, which never found an appropriate outlet.

So at the end Bengt is totally left to himself, free from commitments to past values and principles, since they have all turned their backs on him. Bengt's liberation from the confining value systems is, in other words, passive, rather than the result of his active and conscious effort to stand on his own.

There are several options open to Bengt in the spiritual and social vacuum created by the elimination of father and mother principles. Ahlin outlines them in the epilogue: Bengt may stay away from more disturbing conflicts, he may fall for the rhetoric of a *Führer*, or he may become a Communist, these being the most conspicuous choices for a young man in search of an attitude in the 1930s, the time of Bengt's (and Ahlin's) formative years. The author, however, finds it most likely that Bengt will realize that "there is no solution for man's most deep-seated difficulties" (379): "How will we overcome our disappointment at not having found the superior I with a personal solid basis for values within us? How will we overcome the illusion of liberalism [about absolute man secure in his own right] and yet keep our dignity?" (38). The answer is that man can live with dignity only if he recognizes and accepts the inherent suffering and difficulty of existence. This he achieves only by compromising with his ideals and accepting his imperfect self.

II   Nigella Damascena

A   *The plot: Balance of values*
The main characters in *Jungfrun i det gröna*[11] (*Nigella Damascena*, 1947) are a principal of a folk high school, Sören, his wife, Astrid, and their two student friends, Stig and Maud. Each person is pursuing an ideal which he expects to find through new relationships: Sören with Maud, Astrid with Stig. But ultimately, they experience a change within themselves by accepting the dichotomies between the ideal and reality.

Sören is a frustrated scholar of art history who has ambitions of becoming an author. In his former student, Maud, he believes he has found the right woman to encourage him in his creativity, to bring out the artist in him. She is different from his wife, Astrid, who he claims has never had faith in him. Astrid is living proof of his failure to rise to his ideal. But when he lies in agony in a hotel room feeling his failure as an artist more strongly than ever, it is Astrid's help and love he needs and receives. Lovingly she caresses him and whispers to him her credo about balance between the extremes and the right to live with dignity even though one does not belong to the elite.

This is possible in love and loyalty to another person who is also loyal to you. As she speaks to him, Sören gradually ceases his total rejection of self, and begins to accept himself as the competent but average man he is. He makes a Lutheran decision to continue working in his assigned world, the folk high school, rather than losing his sense of worth in impossible dreams about artistic superiority, a place he is not meant to fill. He returns, reborn into the reality of his limitations.

While Sören has been nurturing his illusions about his self in Maud's admiration of his authority and talent, Astrid has been trying to satisfy a long-felt wish to bear a child by seducing Stig. Stig is, in the beginning, troubled by the conflicts between man as a political and social being and man as a physical and sensual creature. He has become aware of these conflicts by watching them battle within his father. His father first devoted all of his life to political and social activities, but later became a person who sought only sensual satisfaction. Gradually Stig comes to believe that if he finds a woman he can experience as a person as well as a body, he will also find a way to eliminate the tension within him between social man and sensual man and thereby keep from being crushed by this tension like his father.

By the end of the novel, Stig has become the most important character in terms of delivering the author's message. This is indicated structurally in the concluding chapter by the change in point of view, from an impersonal narrator, to Stig in a first-person monologue, in which he articulates his new awareness of self.

He finds his self by understanding his father, through a process of self-realization which is analogous to Maud's finding of her self through greater understanding and acceptance of her mother.

My inner nature offered many solutions [to his difficulties and conflicts]. My father grew instinctive and forgetful. He used defiance and humor. He cultivated his talent to enjoy life. I tried to find comfort in balance. I longed for the cool attitude of irony. . . .

Now I know that personal happiness is possible, in defeat, in balance, in victory. Love makes the happiness possible. If I love and am loved, happiness is possible regardless of whether or not I succeed in the rest. (247)

He understands now that he needs Maud, who knows both about love and suffering, to balance his life between love and work, his personal and social identities.

After this realization he is able to resume the radical socialist approach to existence which he had rejected earlier. He has, however, come to understand that he must not identify his personal life with his social condition but live with them in balance, in a love not indifferent to social reality, but neither exclusively dependent on this reality. His form of balance, Melberg observes resembles Tåbb's reformism in that they are both "a form of inner readiness to accept the imperfection both in terms of personal qualities and social conditions."[12]

III   A Stove of One's Own

A   *The plot: Challenge of social order*

Egen spis (A Stove of One's Own, 1948)[13] is Ahlin's most amusing novel. He sets a couple of go-getters, Herbert Lager and Evelyn Kull, against a family of happily asocial people, including Harry and Sara Lustig (literally, "Funny"). Still, he portrays both groups with humor and love. Herbert Lager, a merchant and pillar of the local Pentecostal Church, aspires to a seat on the city council. He is the founder of the organization "Stormtroupers Against Obscene Graffiti" ("Stormtruppen mot Otuktigt Kludd") which he hopes will further his chances for election. To this end he also plans a raid on the local establishments that sell liquor illicitly to alcoholics prohibited by the authorities from buying it.

Running against Herbert Lager is Thure Fatt, called Alltnog (literally, "Anyhow"). If he can make Harry Lustig sign the oath of Good Templars, he will gain an edge over his competitor.

Harry Lustig himself lives unperturbed by societal designs on his freedom and pleasures. He has only two problems: keeping his dog from being impounded because he has not paid the dog tax, and handling his wife's request for a stove of her own. Harry does not understand her request because he is used to a family life where everything is shared, from odd jobs to illegitimate children.

Harry's wife Sara is tormented by her failure to produce a child because she believes she must do so to be regarded as a real woman and a good wife. Thure Fatt too is plagued by lack of self-confidence and faith in his own worth. He loves Evelyn Kull, a prominent political figure and owner of the town's largest millinery shop, but feels hopelessly inferior to her and does not dare to express his love openly. Instead, he talks about it with one of Harry's nieces, whom he desires but does not love, he thinks, because he has not put her on a pedestal higher than himself.

Evelyn Kull is also wooed by Herbert Lager and a man called The Carrot, an advocate of health foods and outdoor living. Each of them appeals to different aspects of her personality: Herbert to her intellectual and political ambitions and The Carrot to her libido, two conflicting impulses within her. To punish her sensual self, a lower form of consciousness in her opinion, she considers marrying the pedestrian and unattractive Herbert instead of giving in to her lust for The Carrot's wonderful body.

After a series of burlesque events and complications, most of the characters end up in Thure Fatt's kitchen. There they are seized by sudden revelations about themselves and scatter in various directions to pursue their true happiness. Evelyn Kull gives in to The Carrot; Herbert Lager returns to the church and leaves political life and its corrupting features. Thure Fatt realizes that he loves Harry's niece. Harry himself returns to a happy Sara who has learned that she is pregnant and now makes her first gesture toward accepting the family custom of a shared stove.

B *Failure of social values*

Ahlin's protagonists often approach existence intellectually in reasoning with themselves and about others. But they also display a strong sensual feeling for basic, natural pleasures such as eating and love making. Usually there are both intellectual and sensual elements in one character. They may be in conflict as they are in Tåbb when he meets Anna, or they may be integrated as in Britt-Marie of *Cinnamon Girl*. In *A Stove of One's Own*, however, the two protagonists (interestingly enough, with the same initials), each represent one principle: Herbert Lager is the man of reason and organization, Harry Lustig the man of love and pleasure, and inherent contempt for social values.

The difference between them is strikingly demonstrated in their relation to the women of their lives. Harry thinks about Sara in terms of love and pleasures: the food she gives him and the sex they enjoy. (We get, however, many sensuous details about his eating and none about his love making.) Herbert, on the other hand, as he waits for Evelyn Kull to arrive for a date, translates his attraction to her into dreams about merging their two businesses, his shoe store and her millinery. He also ponders the social question of whether there exists obscene graffiti in women's restrooms.

During the pursuit of his career in politics and business, Herbert becomes involved in more and more absurd activities. His scheme to draw out information from Sara turns against him when she insists that without money to buy the liquor she cannot make Harry show her where the illicit bars are located. This forces Herbert to dispatch his "clean" money for sinful purposes, and the more he tries to appear a citizen of law and order, the more he is drawn into corrupting himself. His apparent respectability crumbles as his ambitions carry him away from his basic standards of conduct.

Harry Lustig is corrupt, from a social point of view, because of his bohemian life-style and disrespect for the law regarding dog tax; but he is morally sound. His life is in essence more religious than Herbert's because it is based on fundamental human values: love and humoristic acceptance of life in all its aspects. Therefore he cannot understand Sara's need for a stove of her own, which he thinks is an expression of a socially inspired tendency to put individual ownership above family love — something which does not fit into his value system.

Sara's dream for a stove of her own is, however, an expression for her feeling of being inferior, and worthless, because she is childless. To her, the Lustig family stove symbolizes a life she feels unworthy of, because she has not contributed to its perpetuation.

In her mind, "stove" stands for family and continuation of life, and does not signify allegiance to the social vice of ownership or the need for individual recognition. Harry's confusion on this point gives in to contented realization of the true meaning of the stove when he mulls over the information that he will become a father:

— It looks as if we're going to have a baby, she said. And from that moment it never occurred to Harry to ask anyone advice on the right of a married woman to a stove of her own. . . . People and relatives would also in the future gather around a stove then . . . supervised by Sara and himself. . . . Nature must take its course, he thought. You can do nothing about that. He was happy. (255)

On this note the novel ends. The corrupt ambition and selfishness of the go-getters have been proven less viable values than the love embodied in the Lustig family. Superficially, the go-getters represent desirable social qualities: they are hard working, responsible, and law obeying citizens. For them, the Lustig's easy-going lust for life and pleasure is a disturbing element in their well-organized world, and they do not recognize that the underlying element of love and compassion for all living things is a more fundamental value than organizations and political systems can provide.

The Lustigs and their antisocial value system survive attacks by society because, fundamentally, and consistent with the Christian doctrine which Ahlin espouses, their values are based on love for their neighbor. Society's foremost representatives, Herbert Lager and Evelyn Kull, are most concerned with exploiting their neighbor. The Lustigs' merry attitude to life, which is articulated also in their name, is not hedonism but rather a form of joy for life, defining a sense of harmony between the self and existence in its profane as well as sacred forms.

From society's point of view, Harry Lustig is an alcoholic and welfare case at the very bottom of the social hierarchy. Ahlin transforms this social bum into a philosopher or apostle of love, wandering in a strange world governed by other principles. Harry Lustig's social inferiority is balanced by his spiritual superiority, and in the end his world is shown to be one of order and purpose while the social notion of order has been forced to yield.

In the novels following the six discussed in Chapters 3 and 4, Ahlin focuses less on failure and more on love. In the earlier novels, love is the redeeming factor which renders a person's social evaluation of self irrelevant to his ultimate appreciation of self. In the later novels, the point of view is reversed so that instead of describing how a sense of failure is overcome by love, the writer discusses love and its encounter with failure. The transition between these two perspectives of thematic focus takes place in *Stora glömskan (The Great Amnesia,* 1954), discussed in the following chapter.

CHAPTER 5

The Great Amnesia

I   *The plot: About freedom and the workings of love*

S*tora glömskan (The Great Amnesia,* 1954)[1] was published the year after *Cinnamon Girl.* The setting is Ahlin's fictional Sundsvall in the 1920s. Thirteen-year-old Zackarias wakes up filled with a joy and vitality of almost unbearable intensity which force him out of the house. He needs space to practice his favorite game of walking backward with closed eyes. The game gives him simultaneous sensations of fear and satisfaction: "The law of gravitation is looping capriciously between grace and punishment. . . . Does not another world begin where the raised foot hesitates to step down?" (10). He is brought back to "normal use of the five senses" (11) by Alexis Bring, called AB, a journalist and editor of numerous failing magazines who is plagued by insomnia. His afflication illustrates his lack of "psychic energy"; he is mentally paralyzed and cannot concentrate on work or achievement. Ahlin describes his condition as one without concrete worries, but one in which the world is "grey, unarticulated and mute" (11).

Only Zackarias can eventually bring AB out of this state, but only if his psychic energy and his balance between conscious and unconscious powers are stronger than AB's lack of balance. Zackarias' recent experience of joy indicates that he is now ready to take on the "work" of bringing AB out of his isolation of self, guiding him out of his "spiritual distress" (12) *(själens omkommenhet)* back into relationships with other people. Relating to others is, according to Ahlin's Lutheran-inspired belief, man's ultimate calling and a duty he must not reject.[2]

They walk to a ditch where the ropemaker Master Torkel drowned and AB receives new energy as he stands looking at this spot. Master Torkel had left his clothes and watch on the embankment and stepped into the water as if he were going to bed. This encounter

94

with sleep turned to death transforms AB, who has been trapped in living death through his insomnia. Now AB is ready to work on a new magazine, which means that he can begin to relate to other people.

Zackarias too becomes aware of a strong interaction between life and death:

Everything was alive and I was both afraid and elated. . . . I began to run. A silent joy was streaming from wall to wall. Everything could have been different. I ran. Soon it will be only painful, I thought. How does one dare. . . . So I ran. All that lives must die. Everything could be different. . . . Everything by living human hands. . . . That one dares. (29)

And Zackarias runs to the sunny harbor, revealing that he is beginning to be touched by life's inherent qualities of pain and joy, and the distress which these may bring him.

Together with his friend Thure, Zackarias fetches a cow from a poor farmer who must sell it because he has defaulted on his mortgage payment, spending his money on drink rather than paying it to the bank. Zackarias' father, in partnership with a shady cattle dealer, specializes in "saving" such wretched farmers by buying their cattle at bargain prices. Except for Zackarias' comment, "Saving was their word" (36), his father's questionable business ethics are not morally condemned. The implicit author is more concerned here with the morals of relationships between all God-created beings and man's lack of respect for individual dignity, whether it be toward man or animal. As Zackarias' grandmother observes: "I don't think any city people treat animals right. They have forgotten that. Maybe most people have forgotten it. What are the animals to them? Animals are food. But the food was a living animal. Someone killed the animal, took its life. How do they look upon that act? What do they think?" (38 - 39). She conveys her Lutheran and Pauline view of life as a continuous process of consumption and recreation.[3] Therefore, she says, the butcher, "when he sticks his knife in the sacred and clean animal, ought to say: 'In the name of Christ' and then cross its front hooves and say 'we will meet on the day of Resurrection' " (40). The ritual surrounding the slaughter of animals for food may seem, to an American reader, more inspired by Jewish than Protestant custom, but according to Ahlin it belongs to old Swedish folk custom.[4]

Zackarias remembers his grandmother's words as he helps Thure bring home the cow who refuses to cooperate. Struggling with her, Zackarias falls and in the fall his hand, grasping for support, slips

between the cow's thighs. Touching the cow's soft, warm, moist skin
he perceives, sensually, that the cow is a sacred, divine creation like
himself. Therefore when the cow is slaughtered, he secretly crosses
its hooves and repeats his grandmother's words.

Another of the townspeople, Augustin, drowned some years ago,
but he lives in Zackarias' memory and is symbolically present in a
sunken boat, an object toward which Zackarias sometimes feels
mysteriously drawn. With his friend the bald-headed Ulrik, he sets
out on an excursion through a forest which will lead them to the
boat. A girl, Olga, follows them and Zackarias learns that Ulrik has
said that he will let her caress his baldhead three times.

Ulrik, bald as an old man, singled out from the other children by
his oddity, belongs nowhere and feels as if he is floating in "ice-cold
space surrounded by his impending death" (62). To Olga he is an
object for ritual and mystical detachment from conventional reality.
To Zackarias he illustrates man's helplessness against the unavoidable inequities of life and man's fear of death as a final condition. There is, however, no need for despair, Zackarias thinks,
because: "The name is alive. . . . We are always alive with someone. . . . No one dies alone" (63).

In this respect Augustin is alive in Zackarias' memory in the
sunken boat, and Ulrik tries to capture this eternal life for himself
outside value systems. Therefore he demands that Zackarias dive
down to the boat in his presence before he will let himself be treated
merely as an object of curiosity by Olga, and Zackarias plunges into
the water. After his return to the surface, Zackarias is overwhelmed
by a feeling of intense joy which seems to be a manifestation of a
divine principle of love. Then follows an episode which teaches
about work and love.

Standing in a park with his back against a tree, Zackarias senses a
mystical participation between inanimate and animate creations:
"The tree became dear to me. I was received into its life" (64). And
echoing his feelings is Kacklan, a washer woman, as she lifts her
arms and cries: "The stones should have known" (64). By this ex-
clamation she means that her love for her late husband, Jonsson, had
formed a natural part of her very being, and, though he did not understand it, her love had been as solid as the rocks. And yet she felt
contempt for him, she tells Zackarias.

This may seem paradoxical, but it is a paradox we also find in
God's love. At times, Luther argues, there is an apparent dichotomy
between God's love of man and His display of wrath. His wrath,
however, is not directed toward man, but toward the sin in man.

God hides His true nature of love under a mask of wrath in order to fight against sin.[5] Similarly, Jonsson's moral decay, or sins, had forced Kacklan to hide her love behind a mask of seemingly opposite feelings. She seems an unlikely god figure, in her decrepitude and low class status, but paradoxically, like many of Ahlin's female characters, she embodies fundamental godlike qualities. This Zackarias learns in their next conversation: her husband had frozen to death one night when he came home drunk and she refused to let him into the house. Zackarias asks if she had loved him then too.

— Are you true when you claim that you loved Jonsson those days?
— Yes I am. Didn't I work day and night? Did I refuse to give him his daily bread?
— Is that love?
— What else do you think love is?
— A tender feeling in your heart.
— And then nothing more?
— You show your feelings to your beloved, of course, and then a great deal happens.
— Nonsense Zackarias. To show your feelings. Window displays do not fill your beloved's empty stomach. Clothes in shop windows do not warm you. No, you must work. You work for your beloved. Work is love. I worked day and night.
— Why do people say that God is love?
— He works. Above all, he works. He lets the sun shine. . . . (71)

After his conversation with Kacklan, he meets the woodcutter, Matti, a man "who lived in togetherness with things" (78). Matti is a religious man, though he does not hold institutionalized religion in high esteem. When he goes to church he sits so far back that he cannot hear what the minister says because, in his Kierkegaardian opinion, priests preach their own words and not God's pure words..

In Matti's ever-changing face, Zackarias visualizes life as always changing and yet always the same. In this quality, Zackarias sees a form of equality among people: everyone is subject to the same life regardless of social status.

Matti becomes involved in a plan to rescue his compatriots, a group of Finns, from being sent back to Finland. He devotes himself to this work with such intensity that he frightens Zackarias, making him want to renounce his destiny as a human being.

I did no longer want to be a human being. I wanted to escape the fate of growing up. I wanted to leave my human identity and enter another shape.

A ship? . . . No I asked for invisibility. I asked for even more: no form for me, no substance for me.
I wanted to be an event, something that touches matter and then disappears. (99)

Shortly thereafter Matti dies, after having told Zackarias a tale he has never heard before (nor do we hear it in the book). Now Zackarias understands that Matti was an artist; his life was, by its spiritual qualities, a work of art.

Zackarias is being lent out to a childless couple, Daniel and Emilia Tidewall, who need a child to cure their infertility, according to old Mrs. Fast's remedy. At their house he witnesses strange and inexplicable events.

First he gets to eat a lot of spicy food and then is given a bath and put to bed. Then Emilia wakes her napping husband by moving a burning feather under his nose until he sneezes. When Daniel stands up, both pull out a big chunk of cotton from their underwear while discussing whether or not they have yet acquired "the right temperature."

Zackarias' father explains to him that the only thing wrong with Daniel is that he cannot suffer. "And he who does not suffer, does not love" (144). He must learn to suffer a little, hence the burning feather and the sneezes, before he can father a child, a product of love.

In spite of rituals and occasional "galloping" with Daniel in a rocking chair, Emilia does not become pregnant until, as a last resort, she takes up with Daniel's headman in his shop, following the advice of the old woman. Conventional morality is challenged in this justification for adultery, and ironically, Daniel, who boasts of being totally unprejudiced, becomes a victim, moralistically speaking, of unprejudiced behavior.

One of Ahlin's best satires on institutionalized morals is the next story about Rinaldo Svensson, the teetotaler who must drink himself back to membership in his Good Templar Lodge.

Zackarias' father has, in the eyes of the townspeople, corrupted Rinaldo Svensson into drinking because they are constantly seen together in restaurants. Rinaldo's drinking is, however, an illusion, because in fact both their rations are consumed by Zackarias' father.[6] But with appearances against Rinaldo, his Good Templar Lodge cancels his membership.

This act puts Rinaldo in a difficult situation: his vows are so sacred that he will not consider breaking them by drinking. On the other hand, only as a reformed drinker will he be able to regain his membership in the Lodge. Fortunately, the narrator comments ironically, he is a man devoted to technicalities and he has soon devised a plan which will bring him back into the Lodge without forcing him to drink: he and Zackarias' father are to visit the town's more prominent restaurants and consume maximum allowances of liquor, whereupon Rinaldo will pretend to become more and more drunk even though he of course, as usual, will let Zackarias' father drink it all. Finally he will dispatch a note to his brethren begging to be saved from the curse of drink.

The plan works well except that the lodge first sends one of their low-ranking members, which offends Rinaldo's sense of dignity and self importance: he has, after all, been a faithful member for many years. He thinks he deserves to be saved by the highest ranking officer and refuses to accept any other missionary.

In this story, Zackarias' role is almost exclusively that of observer and narrator. However, in the next section, Zackarias searches for his father and in the process realizes that he cannot remain an observer, or become an event without substance; he must take part in life himself and become part of a system of human relations.

Zackarias' father has disappeared, something he does occasionally, each time disrupting the order in his home. Strange visitors appear, mostly women, and the food is not cooked right. The house undergoes a thorough cleaning and everything is turned upside down, symbolically translating despair into trivial domestic activity. Zackarias' stepmother vacillates between frantic activities and "a dark and still feeling" (170). She denies herself the comfort of giving in to her despair and loneliness and carries on her work in anguish.

Zackarias dreams that his father's life is threatened, but his premonition of danger vanishes when he remembers a visit to the Lapps which he and his father had made shortly before the disappearance. Inspired by the horns of the reindeers, Zackarias had then envisioned a primeval merging of animate and inanimate worlds. This had taken place, he believes, one time when the reindeer had sensed "the tree's sorrow" at being confined to the same place. The animal had then "bent its head and a secret union between animal world and plant world had taken place" (176). This had made him realize that there are other worlds than the one we see, and this notion of a multifaceted existence now brings him comfort. He understands that his father does not have to be in danger, even though he cannot be found or seen.

Next Zackarias meets Sam Andersson, called "The Great

Amnesia" ever since he returned from the United States and had to
ask directions to even the best-known places of his home town. He
leads a good life because he has made himself independent of man-
created features of existence and can live *in* the world without living
from the world and its notion of what is important and what is not,
its values and hierarchies. He is free to be anywhere in his mind, and
can therefore, Zackarias tells us, exist in two places simultaneously
without rejecting the place where his body is, even though it may be
inferior to the dwelling of his mind.

Zackarias asks "The Great Amnesia" to tell him something about
his wife, and this leads to a change of Zackarias' perspective on self:

I looked up at him. Sam had received an invisible visitor. I had to close my
eyes and I think that I in that moment smiled the way "The Great Amnesia"
could smile. My distant future stepped out and embraced me. Something
happens in the dark room and I feel how I am being formed to live with
someone. A woman's voice is calling for me. And I know how to walk and
how I want to use my hands. (191)

After this experience he is better equipped to trace his lost father
because he has acquired a new sense of relationship with others. But
his trials are not yet over. As his earlier wish to become invisible and
without substance is replaced with his new sense of form, he is interrupted by Engelbrekt Palm, a candy maker, businessman, and dis-
agreeable acquaintance of his father.

Though Palm knows where the father is, he refuses to tell
Zackarias anything and keeps him guessing, gloating about his
power over Zackarias' mind and feelings. Instead of the information
Zackarias wants, he offers him the opportunity to earn money wrapping candy in his kitchen and Zackarias accepts, hoping to learn
something about his father.

Zackarias and Palm mirror each other's situations: Zackarias is a
son in search of his father; Palm is a father expecting his son's birth.
He is, in a Jungian sense, the shadow of Zackarias' father in that he
embodies the father's negative qualities. Palm is always business
minded to the detriment of his humanness; he is conniving and unreliable. By working for him, Zackarias is going through the type of
ordeal heroes of tales must confront before they reach their goal: he
must work for the "troll," that is, learn to handle the negative
qualities of life and man in order to mature. As he sits wrapping
candy for Palm he feels psychologically as if he is in hell, and his
despair grows:

When, does he ask himself, will we learn to live with our limits:
After the returns.
After the return from our passion's union with God.
After the return from our despair's union with Satan. (208)

In spite of his dislike for Palm, Zackarias knows he will return to work because Palm is, after all, his only source of information about the father. The next time he sits wrapping the candy, his thoughts focus on his father's attitude toward death:

To Dad life was fun and spontaneous actions, always entertainment or lack of it. Somewhere he was always bleeding. Dad was a friend of death. To die was to him more like taking off your clothes and lying down to sleep. . . To die meant to him to be able to hope anew to take off everything that had become worn and destroyed and to believe in a new morning of creation. (224)

His father's disappearance, Zackarias is beginning to understand, is such a death and he will therefore return. In this new mood of optimism he meets "The Great Amnesia" again, and is filled with joy and self-confidence. Moreover, aside from wanting to find his father, he wants to hear "The Great Amnesia" speak about love. He comes to understand that love unites two radically different principles, male and female, and this represents cosmic harmony. Without this union the world is not functioning properly; therefore, as long as Zackarias' father is absent from home and wife, Zackarias' world is in disorder. His search, in other words, is not only a search for the father but an attempt to recapture lost order. Suddenly and without drama he meets his father on the street returning from a visit with the Lapps.

After a bath and change of clothes, the father returns home. His wife and a bed with clean sheets are waiting for him, and from the next room Zackarias hears his parents' joyous laughter as he drifts off to sleep, back to the same state of consciousness in which we found him in the beginning of the novel.

II *Structure*

Narrative coherence is created by the same Joycean playfulness with the language we found in *If, About, Around.* The seemingly loosely connected stories are in fact conceived with a much tighter formal pattern than one usually perceives at first reading.

Toward the end of the first story "Master Torkel's Ditch,"

Zackarias is running toward the harbor with random thoughts tumbling in his head. Though disjointed in a narrative sense, they are coherent in that they refer to social features: houses, streets, institutions, except for the question "Did no one meet the crazy elephant?" (29). This apparently out-of-place statement is explained a few pages later: As Zackarias stands waiting for his friend Thure at the "Hayscale" ("Hövågen"), he recalls a time when a circus passed through and had to weigh their elephants on the "Hayscale." Naturally he could come to think about the elephant while he was standing by the "Hayscale," but why the elephant in the first story?

The two elephants are connected in Zackarias' mind through a process similar to the one which takes place in dreams where, to use Freudian terminology, condensation and displacement of words or events create new rules of logic not inhibited by the rationality of the wakened consciousness. This leads to a situation where the result of an event or the conclusion of a train of thought may be placed at the beginning of a dream and its premises at the end.[7] As in a dream, Zackarias' associations call forth the first elephant by connecting "dare" (vågar) from his original stream of thoughts (how does one dare?) with "the scale" (vågen, plural vågar) where he first saw an elephant. Ahlin seems to be working with this kind of narrative unity in all of the novel's first stories, a very illustrative method to indicate Zackarias' freedom from ordinary conventions and to imply that he is living both in a physical world and a dream, or subconscious world.

In addition to the use of "dream structure" as the basis for narrative structure, there is a cinematic type of unifying device between the sections. A "sound dissolve" carries the transition between the first three stories: playing his backward walking game, Zackarias suddenly remembers hearing bellowing seals fighting to the death. The bellowing resounds then from the obstinate cow dragged away by Thure and Zackarias; and a similar sound is heard when the mother bellows after Olga, the girl who followed Ulrik and Zackarias through the forest.

Olga herself provides another form of structural unity through her sensual touching of Ulrik's baldhead, displaying similar emotional energy to Zackarias' earlier sensual pleasure as his hand slid between the cow's thighs.

The idea of struggle and animal ties in with Kacklan's difficulty with her wheelbarrow, which reminds Zackarias of a struggle with an obstinate animal. The stories are also linked by other elements from nature: the forest in one story becomes a grove of poplar trees in the next, with leaves shimmering like a school of fish; and the trees then change into the wood which Matti handles. As Zackarias' consciousness awakens through experience, nature becomes more civilized and turns into a form man can handle and touch with his hands. As nature becomes more articulated and identified, Zackarias grows more aware of life's many aspects.

In the final section, "It is getting warmer," characterization provides the unity with the earlier parts. "The Great Amnesia" is a composite character, to use another Freudian concept,[8] created from the good of the good characters: Kacklan's love, Matti's faces, Augustin's and Master Torkel's timelessness. Engelbrekt Palm, then, is the composite character of the bad in other characters, sterile in mind as Daniel is sterile in body, corrupted by his misplaced sense of value like Rinaldo, possessing his father's negative aspects.

The dreamlike mood from the beginning of the book is intensified toward the end, with its mixture of dream sensations, visions, and premonitions. In his dream consciousness, Zackarias does not experience only pleasant and joyous events. Despair and death exist also in his "other" reality and, as he runs through the town looking for his father, he learns that physical reality and "dreams" are both interdependent and equally important to his total identity.

III *The father and other authority figures*

The father represents play and games, irregularity and disorder, wisdom and freedom from conventions. He offers Zackarias neither conventional stability nor social ideal with which to identify, but he teaches him that spiritual harmony comes when one senses a cosmic unity between different forms of existence, when a man is free from the restrictions of social conditioning in his view of self. Zackarias responds to his father's multifaceted nature with a wide range of feelings, from reverence for his sagacity to fear for his death. Thus he, like Bengt in *If, About, Around*, simultaneously regards his father as an authority to look up to and a person to protect.

This ambivalence in Zackarias' attitude reflects his mixed feelings about himself. At first he fears growing up and being subject to the inherent changes of life. Gradually, however, he comes to accept the conditions of existence and its many faces which he sees represented in the faces of Matti and "The Great Amnesia," the true father figures.

Matti and "The Great Amnesia" have one social occupation and many faces, while the father has one face and many social occupations. He is a jack-of-all-trades, some of them not very acceptable from a moralistic point of view. The father, like Peter in *If, About, Around*, represents the corruptibility of society. But he also represents, like the other father figures, the spiritual freedom gained by rejecting the validity of social standards.

The father appears only occasionally in the first five stories: he helps Zackarias put his experience of joy in the right perspective. He colors everyday life with his imagination: the exposure of the nature of his partnership with the cattle dealer turns into skit, a pantomime, which makes any moral evaluation of his business ethics appear petty and irrelevant. He is, however, not absolutely immoral. Like Matti, the father finds it objectionable that the minister's office divides up people into herd and shepherd, thereby implying differences of value and importance between them. In other words, institutions, not people, are immoral.

Except for Staffan Hyrell in *Tåbb with the Manifesto*, the wisdom of Ahlin's father figures is gained through experience and not intellectually acquired. Matti is a woodcutter, a simple man, yet embodying the highest spiritual qualities. He reminds us of the God characters in Lagerkvist's work who are often portrayed as simple and humble old men busy at simple work. There is, for example, great similarity in conception between the God-woodcutter in *The Eternal Smile* and Matti. In *Cinnamon Girl*, a trash collector consoles Britt-Marie in her despair and disorientation. In *A Stove of One's Own*, an old man, "Uret" ("The Watch"), puts time right for people and promotes Harry Lustig's final happiness and harmony.

These helpers of the protagonist function like the archetypal wise old men and women of tales. Ahlin's most unforgettable characters of this type are usually women. We meet, for example, Kacklan in *The Great Amnesia*, Paulina in *Night in the Market Tent*, and Lotten in *Bark and Leaves*.

Though it is not always specified in the texts, the characters give us an impression of being old. Perhaps this is because, as Örjan Lindberger says in his review of *The Great Amnesia*, "Man's purpose and fate is to be worn out and broken down. Ahlin has found that by describing this process he can demonstrate his humaneness. Therefore these old men and women radiate comfort and faith. . . ."[9] They have reached their desirable states of spiritual equilibrium by shedding their individuality and becoming like each other, yet retaining their distinctions in their names.

Their personalities are not dependent upon a specific environment or time or, for that matter, the context of any particular novel; they can easily trade places. They have, to quote Gunnar Brandell, acquired "a sort of impersonal identity which to him [Ahlin] is both bliss and religion." This impersonality allows them to meet life "constantly recreated."[10] They exist, in other words, undisturbed by considerations created by social and cultural needs, and as such they represent Ahlin's ideal for man.

IV   *The nature of joy*

When Zackarias' dreamworld lingers in his consciousness as a sensation of joy, he is more than usually aware of an "other" existence, different from physical reality and its limitations by time, space, and reason. The *joy* is both a sensory and sensual phenomenon:

While I myself was sleeping a "joy spinner" had been awake and unceasingly performed his work within me. Thanks to this enigmatic helper I had been permitted to gain the knowledge of how it feels to be the hero and favorite child of the dreamworlds. I could probably not assimilate further success. The joy became at last so overwhelming that it finally woke me up, and then I felt something resembling the sensation of solemn lust often born when, after a deep dive with open eyes and hands stretched upward, one gradually rises toward a playfully sunny water surface. I smiled and soon discovered how hard I had grasped on to the bed with one hand and the cover with the other. Something threatened to lift and depart from me. (7)

Joy has many qualities. It has form in personifications as "joy spinner" and "helper." *Joy* has magical powers: it moves Zackarias from one reality to another; it is related to both sun and water, two archetypally fundamental elements in man's mythical imagination. *Joy* is at the same time like a spirit which can leave Zackarias' body and even take him along.

The feeling of true *joy* is, in fact, so special that Zackarias must watch out for false sensations of *joy*. The emotional excitement can be deceptive, his father warns: "Was it only happy, or, perhaps blessed dreams? If that was the case the intoxication would disappear. . . . If, on the other hand, the joy spinner had succeeded in creating a lasting mood or maybe even rejuvenated my soul and my body . . . (8). Here *joy* has the highest degree of emotional intensity while more conventionally high-charged words, *happy, blessed,* are downgraded in comparison to *joy.* By this reversal of the conventional scale of values, Zackarias' father emphasizes the extraordinary quality of *joy.* This quality is further enhanced by the notion of *joy* as rebirth, as change of consciousness. Such change was defined in Ahlin's earlier novels in terms of death.

The concept of *joy* is expressed in a more metaphoric language than death, thus making it more of a poetic experience than an intellectual one. For example, when Zackarias and AB walk together, talking about Master Torkel, Zackarias first feels caught in AB's depression. But this does not last long; his joy is stronger than AB's mood: "The joy from the morning was not that easily toppled" (13). This physically vivid description of the *joy* sensation makes it into an object, and Zackarias himself into a container, an image analogous to the theological concept of man as a vessel for the soul; thus *joy* becomes another word for soul or spiritual self.

Joy also has other physical properties. When Zackarias succeeds in communicating with AB, their spiritual contact makes *joy* into *warmth:* "A warmth vibrated between our faces." It also gives it *weight:* "I was filled with heavy joy" (27). *Warmth* establishes a connection between *sun* and *joy.* And as the *warmth* is created between them and Zackarias is filled with *joy,* the *joy* acquires a liquid quality and further developed in other metaphors creating an analogy between *water* and *joy* and *sun:* "Silent joy was streaming from wall to wall" (29); "A streaming wave of joy" (43).

Imagination and reality, the supernatural and the physical worlds, are fused when Zackarias ascends from his dive to the sunken boat and reexperiences his dream sensations of *warmth* and *joy* as he lies on a rock in the sun: "Suddenly I feel the warmth. It is streaming through my body from inside and out. It is a sweet and clean heat. The fire of life. It grinds; it forces something out of me. My whole body becomes new. I am lying here burning. Not consumingly. I am burning with joy to possess my body and to be alive" (62). The *warmth* he feels leads to joy in a series of words suggesting progressively increasing heat: *warmth, heat, fire, burning* to the metaphor I *am burning with joy;* the notion of *movement* this implies is further supported by the notion that the *warmth* "is streaming," like *water,* through his body.

This moving quality of *joy* indicates that the experience of *joy* brings about a change of Zackarias' consciousness. In the later part of the novel, *movement* temporarily replaces *joy* to describe Zackarias' growth of consciousness. Thus, for example, his worries about his father's disappearance are quieted when he recalls an experience of *movement* he had shared with his father. He had seen a herd of reindeer: "Not only the plain mass of grey brown bodies made such a powerful impression. Remarkable to watch was the floating and collective movement. . . . The wholeness you saw running. Like a raft. . . . The herd's movement was a water movement. On the ground such a sliding stream opened the locks to the supernatural" (176). The *movement* leads from the immediate world to the transcendental and connects the animal world with man's world. Here Zackarias is beginning to realize that there is a uniting factor inherent in all creation. This factor is associated with *water*, the origin of life: the reindeer move *like water*, the dive in the beginning is movement *in water*, and Zackarias' first sensation of joy is a feeling of ascension *from water*.

Reality and dream experiences merge as his actions and thoughts are repeated or relived in each form of existence. The sensation from the first dream is recreated when he actually ascends from his dive to the sunken boat. Likewise, though in reversed order, physical reality occurring before the vision, the reindeer scene from reality, is repeated in a dreamlike situation:

Then I saw the reindeer herd come. It appeared behind a barren mountain ridge and ran down a desolate hill. I could not see any individual animal. It was the herd as such that was running down the stone grey hill. The movement was a water movement. . . .
Oh, I wanted to stop this movement. . . .
The herd came closer. . . .
Then I saw the herd at a distance again. The individual animals had melted together into a herd and the water movement carried them on to areas I could not behold. (253 - 54)

As his vision ends Zackarias hears his stepmother, now rejoined with the father, laugh: "Now she laughed from her own joy and father echoed her" (254). This marks the end of the novel. *Joy, movement,* and *water* are brought together in a unifying experience between father and mother, husband and wife, man and woman. Order is restored, the world is reborn.

As Zackarias experiences various manifestations of the *joy* principle, his consciousness of self grows. His wish in the beginning to become an event, to be without form or identity, is replaced near the end by his vision of belonging to a woman, of hearing a woman call for him. By thus accepting his need for a relationship with a female counterpart, he has gained substance and identity, which, according to Ahlin, we have only in relating to others, particularly in a male-female relationship. When Zackarias falls asleep and returns to the spiritual world which contained his *joy* in the beginning, he hears *joy* has now become part of his existence in the physical world as well, and in this existence, *joy* is part of love.

CHAPTER 6

Four Novels on Love

I *Unconditional love*

AHLIN'S readings on the subject of love during the formative years before his debut include Anders Nygren's *Eros and Agape*, which made a great impression on him, and writings by Luther and St. Paul.[1] Nygren argues that man finds a "good life" only through God's love, *agape*, which is given to everybody regardless of merit or rank.[2] *Agape* creates worth in its object by regarding "as very precious the thing that is loved," Luther says in *Lectures on Romans*.[3] Furthermore, *agape* acts spontaneously and is "unmotivated," Nygren explains, and in this respect differs from human love, which looks for recognized value in its object. While human love is dependent on socially created worth in its object, *agape* stands indifferent to any other notion of worth but love itself.[4]

Agape also relates unconditionally to its object and expects nothing in return for its gift of love.[5] God, by so loving man, shows him how he should love his neighbor. As Nygren claims, when Christ decreed that "you shall love your neighbor just like yourself," he meant our neighbor, just as he is, in "his actual situation and within his actual qualities, not a construed ideal image, not God in him."[6]

Similarly, our love of God should be unconditional, Luther explains, because true love of God is a matter of faith since we cannot know Him empirically. This love:

is the purest feeling toward God and alone makes us right at heart, alone takes away inequity, alone extinguishes the enjoyment of our righteousness. For it [this love] loves nothing but God alone, not even His gifts as the hypocritical self-righteous people do. . . . we love God alone, where nothing is visible, nothing experiential, either inwardly or outwardly, in which we

109

can trust or which is to be loved or feared, but it is carried away beyond all things into the invisible God, who cannot be experienced, who cannot be comprehended, that is, into the midst of the shadows, not knowing what it loves, only knowing what it does not love (Luther, 294).

There is, in other words, no social reward for this love because it is not directed toward a socially definable or rankable object, and therefore it cannot reflect back to us and increase our social value in our own or society's eyes. Instead, we must commit ourselves totally in love, and this commitment is our reward.

This does not mean that love is blind to faults and inadequacies in the loved one. On the contrary, Nygren declares, judgment of the beloved is implicit in true love, but it is a question of judging man with love: "Only the love that judges all that is not love is a profoundly creative and saving love."[7] Therefore, God's love of man is also expressed in His wrath toward man, as Luther never tires of explaining.[8]

II   Love of our neighbor

Man's love of his neighbor should be without illusions; that is, man should not seek ideal qualities in his object, but he should recognize and condemn that which is corrupt and degrading to self and yet love his neighbor in totality.

The quality of man's love of others depends upon whether or not he is inspired by *agape*, because the origin of love, rather than the value of its object, defines its quality and worth.[9] The love which is created from external attraction and social desirability of the object is "desirous" and ultimately selfish, while *agape* is totally unselfish and regards social virtues as *adiaphora* (non-consequential) and therefore irrelevant in a relationship of love.[10] We do not love, Luther declares, if we "use each good for ourselves"; we love only when we use it for our neighbor and forget ourselves and our own pleasures. Love, not satisfaction of self, becomes our primary concern in our relations with others. Therefore we can say that love "begins with itself," meaning that it does not seek social success or merit, or ask for emotional rewards. Instead, love means that we are content to serve our neighbor, and to seek his good. By so doing, man in fact "loves himself outside himself," thus fulfilling his calling in this world which is his only way of expressing his love of God.[11]

III   *Uniting love*

Luther describes the unifying quality of love by stating that love is a "unifying force which makes the loved and the lover into one."[12] When God in his love for man became Christ, we understand that He enabled man to love "himself outside himself," making him simultaneously the subject of, and object for, love. This is accomplished in man's love of his neighbor which is a function of his love for Christ who is man, our neighbor, and still God. Man is then the lover of Christ as God and simultaneously the loved one in Christ as man. This unites man and God in love and ultimately man with himself. Through this process man overcomes "the disunion in which [he] lives," says the modern theologian Bonhoeffer[13] and thereby his own alienation and despair.

The unifying power originates with God because man, Bonhoeffer explains, cannot in his "existence in disunion" create a sense of unity in this world by himself. God, however, transforms man's existence through love expressed in the Christ figure so that he is "drawn into the world as it lives and must live." The transformation enables man to direct his love toward others who share his existence in this world.

IV   *Paradox of love*

In addition to being a unifying force, love is paradoxical in its relation to self: "true love for yourself is hatred of yourself," Luther says,[14] as it is in relation to life: "Whoever loves his life will lose it and he who hates his life will find it" (Mark 8:35). Here we assume "life" means, on the one hand socially made values, ideals, and systems, and on the other hand individual values created for each man in the love of each man.

The paradox of love lies also in the fact that love, though a highly desirous state of existence, does not always bring man undisturbed bliss: it often brings pain instead. Because "love is the pleasure in someone else . . . it enjoys the beloved," as Luther says,[15] it is willing to suffer for the beloved. The connection between love and suffering is of particular importance to Luther who sees "the cross and sufferings"[16] as necessary consequences of love, without which the soul would become "lazy and tepid." Suffering does not diminish the joy of love. Instead, suffering constitutes an active part of the total love experience and strengthens man's character, for love "does not seek its own" as St. Paul says in his First Epistle to the Corinthians (13:5):

"It will bear anything, believe anything, hope for anything, endure anything."[17]

Love, we conclude, is not a consuming power which feeds on already existing virtues and qualities. Instead, it gives all good to its object, even though it may entail suffering for the lover; and so love, paradoxically, finds joy in pain.

V   Love and the world

In both novels and essays,[18] Ahlin emphasizes that man must learn to live and love in this world, and not escape from his given reality into metaphysics or unrealistic longings to reach impossible ideals. One of Ahlin's sources for this Lutheran view of the nature and purpose of man's relation to the world is probably Wingren's Luthers lära om kallelsen (Luther's Teachings About Man's Calling),[19] a treatise on man's responsibility to the world as expressed in his work: "The deeds and the calling, that is, love is for the world and our neighbor, not for eternity and God, for He does not need our deeds but our neighbor does. God wants our faith."[20] Nor does God need our love, because He is love; but this world needs it and we express it in our work for others.

There is, Wingren explains, no law for how man shall express his love, but he must seek the form that best serves his neighbor in his particular existence. If love becomes a law, or if the expression of love becomes a matter of law, it ceases to be love.[21] The emphasis on work as a form of love places love in everyday life where it belongs. This removes it from the realm of ideals which only give man feelings of inferiority since he, by definition, cannot become one with his ideal.

Striving for ideals turns man away from his responsibilities in the world and to his neighbor. To direct man's love downward to the world in which he must live, with all its and his own imperfections, God became man in Christ, thus deglorifying His divine nature to help man live according to his human nature. By loving and serving his neighbor through work as best he can, given his powers and talents, man fulfills his calling as a human being. This should be sufficient satisfaction for him.

But man is not satisfied with such individual manifestations of love, because his social conditioning compels him to love only what has worth in social terms. He therefore measures his love against a value system and accepts it only if it ranks high in the hierarchy of societal values. He does not question that love itself is the "highest" of principles, but he fails to recognize its own true value without attaching it to values already established. Thus, by so doing man perpetuates his feelings of inferiority and worthlessness, and not until he liberates himself from the "laws" imposed upon his consciousness by extrapersonal agencies can he truly love and accept being loved. In the process, man must suffer from his own misconceptions of the nature of self, the purpose of his existence as it relates to society, and his ideals and the ultimate value of his collectively created social values.

VI   *Love and sex*

Ahlin often expresses his characters' failure to separate love from social evaluations of self, in the quality of their sexual relations. Misery of the soul caused by feelings of social failure makes his characters incapable of loving or receiving love, and this they react to physically; the sexual act becomes a degrading or grotesque experience. This happens, for example, in *My Death Is My Own* when Sylvan makes love to Engla in the forest, and in the rocking chair and forest group sex episodes in *Pious Murders*. A character's fulfillment of love, on the other hand, is reflected in profoundly satisfying sex. The sexual act symbolizes spiritual harmony and a sense of unity of self, as if the disunion of the world, at the moment of sexual union, were eliminated, and the wholeness of original creation recaptured.

Ahlin's characters do not often experience this perfect existence in the present. For example, Tåbb and Kajsa in *Tåbb with the Manifesto* will, we surmise, first meet in such communications of love in the future. Also in the implied future lies the perfection in love through sex for the father and the mother in *The Great Amnesia*, as they enter their bed upon the father's return at the end of the novel. But for Paulina in *Night in the Market Tent*, to be discussed in this chapter, such expression of love lies in memories of the past.

VII   *Summary*

In Ahlin's novels, love, like death, is a force which creates equality between people, because differences established in a hierarchical social structure become unimportant in love which does not seek socially generated forms of value ·in its object. Instead, love gives value to a person, regardless of how lowly and inferior he appears in terms of social status. Nor is love negatively affected by a person's failure to comply with his own expectations, whether in terms of his social image or his personal relationship. This is so because love, as Ahlin understands it, is inspired by *agape*, God's unconditional love of man. It is, as Luther explains, a function of man's love of God which God wills that he direct to his fellow man. We conclude from this that man needs his neighbor's love, as a counterweight to social inequities and personal inadequacies, in order to keep a sense of human dignity.

In the following four novels Ahlin describes man's way of achieving understanding of his true value, and thereby understanding the true nature of love.

VIII   Woman Woman

A   *The plot: The process of individuation*

Torgny Larsson, a newly married construction worker, has at his wife's exhortations left their little farm in the woods to work in a coastal town to bring home some money.[22] His wife, Ester, owns the farm, while he owns only his body and his working skill. His lack of material possessions makes him feel inferior and he therefore gives in to her will, although he would have preferred to stay with her and build their own house away from her old father's house where they had lived.

He is hardly settled in his work before she begins to haunt him in his sleep like a nightmare, arousing him, challenging him to a competition of wills, making him want to leave at once to go back to show her that his will is equal to hers. But he also needs her emotionally and does not know how to integrate this need for her with the power struggle between their wills. He wants to confront her at once to demonstrate his independence and strength through disobedience; however, one part of him is insecure about his right to demand equal voice in their relationship as long as he has no money or property.

Before he finally decides whether to leave his new job, he meets a number of men who present him with the vision of a life of freedom from women, independence instead of marriage, adventure instead of work. The first man is Olaus Skruv (literally, "Screw") who got his name from the day a woodscrew was accidentally shot into his head, and remained there visible to the world. He began making money as a curiosity, a freak, by letting people scratch the screw with a knitting needle creating an eerie sound which conjured up a sensation of both delight and fear.

Torgny ponders borrowing money from Skruv. But before he turns to Skruv, he portrays his feelings of inferiority in a bitter soliloquy about the materialism of women:

He must throw gold on the scale if it is to balance in his favor. Before the power of money, women's resistance melts and she yields. She does not dare to challenge the man who jingles money. He is the master of his house. . . . I love my woman uncle Olaus, I must go to her. Now, now. Hear, hear how she with all women in all times joins the eternal cry: money, money, money. (86 - 87)

However, at the last moment he drops the idea. He is suddenly seized with disgust for the world of women and soon he dreams about freedom — "Men's freedom" (88). There is, as Artur Lundkvist commented in his review, something of Strindberg's view of marriage in this presentation of woman as a dominant, money-hungry demon.[23] There also appears to be something of Hemingway in this dream of a world without women — women who represent social responsibility and restrictions for the free male spirit.

Drawn thus to the world of men, Torgny loiters in the harbor, soaking up its flavor and activities. But sometimes he feels "the wind from woman's world" (122), and Ester ceases to threaten him with her overpowering will and instead turns into a sensual dream image: "He caressed her kneecap. His hands were thirsty for them. . . . They were smooth and sleek and hard like cobblestones. . . . How could his hands worship these knees so deeply? Had they not made other discoveries on her body? Yes, they had. Yet his hands preferred these kneecaps" (122).

He soon realizes that the male world is not all virility and freedom from conflicts. The narrator next provides two tales from which Torgny also learns about the vulnerability, weakness, and restrictions inherent in the male nature. He hears the story about Alvar who lost his manhood when he began baking bread. This tale describes the archetypal castrating powers of the female, a power different from the one Ester has exerted over Torgny. The tale deals with the danger for man of witnessing or partaking of the female mysteries: baking, brewing, and cooking, as described by Erich Neumann in *The Great Mother*.

The female principle in the tale about Alvar is devouring and dangerous. Woman's power over man's sexuality is portrayed as destructive rather than creative, and it balances Torgny's sensual longing for Ester by pointing out the potential effect of becoming too engrossed in the nature of woman. At the same time, the tale indicates that Ester's more devastating power lies not in her material goods but in her physical nature, and in this realm of existence Torgny is superior; he brought to their marriage "his strong body." He has now been told that his power is equal to hers, even though they are manifested in different forms — money versus body.

Next Torgny is arm wrestling with Gullrik Thörngren, an embodiment of supermasculine virtues. It is as if Torgny were wrestling with the male principle rather than an ordinary man, as if his psychological balance rather than his arm muscles were being tested. Gullrik's world offers him a simple existence ruled by simple forces — muscles in place of mysteries, where worth is easily defined as force, uncomplicated by emotions and cultural values.

Torgny wins over Gullrik and thereby conquers his doubts about his own worth in Ester's eyes and his fear of her power over him. He will not come to her as the epitome of one-sided manliness demanding to be her master and superior. Nor will he yield to her, insecure in his own worth. He has felt her inside him, learned of her powers, rejected his own longing for freedom in a simple but incomplete male existence, and now he can meet her in love, his strength equal to hers. He no longer perceives his longing for her as a weakness, but rather a natural consequence of his love for her.

Having come to this realization, Torgny begins his forty-mile journey home to Ester, his steps spelling out his new concept of love: "Love destroys all demands. The image man has made of himself outside love is destroyed . . ." (244). "His steps sing 'demand and love, law and gospel'" (247).

B *Judgment in love*

Torgny's reunion with Ester will begin a new relationship because he can now see himself as her equal. Whereas before he was intimidated by her social advantages over him, he now sees that they relate to each other in love, not in social competition. Therefore, he can be judged only by his love, through his love, and only for the qualities that are in conflict with his love.

This new awareness of self he calls having "doomsmood" (*domsmod*) a palindrome signifying that the judgment of love works from two directions — subject and object are interchangeable. Torgny's doomsmood is first described in a "dialogue" between himself and the narrator, as the point of view vascillates between a monologue by Torgny and a detached narrator's comments on him and his doomsmood:

> I knew all the time how to act, he insisted. I only had to test my powers in various ways. In fact, the purpose of my inner struggle was to gain a proper doomsmood. I needed and finally acquired this. Doomsmood, he cried out loudly and clearly as he was running down the highway. For he was alone and the night was light and he rejoiced. Doomsmood, doomsmood rang out like a church bell which summons one to Thanksgiving; then too it was a Holy Scripture and a confession. Doomsmood. Is there in the entire language a more splendid word for a man with a living conscience? Read the word forward or backward, either way is equally correct. . . . Doomsmood is a perfect word. It contains energy. He who truly dares to take it in his mouth is girded with strength. Doomsmood. To hell with you, Torgny Larsson, or to heaven. To a right life or a wrong one. Now I have doomsmood, Ester. (93 - 94)

Torgny is going home because he feels that Ester's decision that he leave was not dictated by love but by materialism. He is now challenging her decision and at the same time placing his decision to be tested by her love. Liberated from the power of her socially oriented will, he is ready to pass judgment over her: "I have doomsmood. In my heart there is a judge. He knows your guilt and tells you that in plain and clear words. In my heart there is also another man. He has already forgiven you. Now it is your turn to do the same for me. Say that you want to live with me just as I am" (241). Still there is a trace of doubt in him until he turns and looks at the city he has just left. The city, a manifestation of society and man-created values, seems to dissolve and with it Torgny's last feelings of inferiority. He is now ready to meet Ester in a creative relationship which is not based on a contest between wills of strength of reason, but on mutual self-giving in love.

IX   Night in the Market Tent

A   *The plot: An education in love*

Natt i marknadstältet (Night in the Market Tent, 1957)[24] is Ahlin's most magnificent work on love. The novel presents numerous characters, typical of Ahlin, with an element of the grotesque in their appearance and destiny. We learn about them from stories inserted, as Nielsen observes, at times when problems arise for the characters, which serve to comment on or explain these situations.[25]

Leopold, Paulina's husband, had left home when he was denied a position as janitor of the local athletic club because he felt humiliated and rejected by his peers. He has returned home on the night the German counsel's villa burns down, and it is during this night that the main events of the novel take place, although there are numerous flashbacks and stories digressing from the main plot.

Leopold had gone away to seek success in the world because, as he had told Paulina: "I seek what I lack. The good. You know that. And the good is always outside. Therefore I cannot remain at home. . . . I do not lack *my* good. If I did I would have stayed with you because you always give me my good. No, *your* good is what I lack and seek" (16). Misunderstanding the essence of love, he believes that material substance, money, or social status are better indices of his worth than the fact that Paulina loves him in the spirit of *agape* and needs no social confirmation of his worthiness to love him. While he seems unselfish from a worldly point of view, his attitude is self-righteous in that he puts conditions on their relationship without considering her feelings.

This need to present her with possessions, to earn her love, saddens Paulina who is totally indifferent to social values in her appreciation of others. She lives humorously,[26] meaning that she finds value in the lowliest forms without denying the fact that they may, from another point of view, seem worthless. She looks upon life from two perspectives simultaneously, and although Leopold is weak and a failure in terms of his worldly attainments,

She not only loved him. She also saw his value and respected him highly. Toward him she was humoristic. . . . The world is bigger than you think. No mathematician can figure out a person's pluses and minuses. But I, she said, I know the sum of you. . . . But he believed that love put lies in her mouth. And he mistrusted her ability to desire *and* renounce, to rejoice *and* suffer, to greet the day *and* sigh with gratitude over the night. You cannot raise something without lowering something else. He found it unjustifiable to raise and lower the same thing alternatingly. Therefore he detested humor. There are not two different kinds of truths as the humorists think. (7)

When he was young, Leopold still had hopes for success and was able to seek comfort from his disappointments and failures in Paulina's arms. His social identity became irrelevant in their relationship where they identified each other only as lovers by the name "Darling" which, unlike their personal names, had no social connotations of success or failure attached to them. Gradually, however, the disgrace of being socially inadequate and unaccepted had made him emotionally inadequate to the extent that he could not make love to Paulina as before. Therefore he had left.

Now Paulina sits alone thinking about how man's individual physical nature commits him to relationships impossible for him to escape:

What do you believe? That man's life is only an invisible and fickle thing, a breeze, a wind, a puff of air behind your back? Oh, no, one does not simply get a man who merely comes and goes. Something called love emerges and becomes inescapable as the wall of a cell. It is not only so that you have children, who run away from you as soon as they can. Something called motherhood comes with it and becomes inescapable as the wall of a cell. (19)

By failing to realize that their love lies at the core of their very being, Leopold rejects its enduring value in favor of shallow and temporary social values. After this background information on Paulina and Leopold, the novel focuses on Zackarias, the boy from *The Great Amnesia*.

One of Zackarias' habits is to hang around the county hospital and talk to the newly discharged patients while they are waiting for their trains home. This is how he meets Klara, who has just been released after attempting suicide. She tells her life story to a sympathetic Zackarias, who responds more maturely than one would expect from a thirteen-year-old boy. He seems intellectually ageless, but he feels uncomfortable about his emotional reaction to Klara's warmth and womanliness, which at the same time attract and frighten him.

Klara is a seemingly vital and happy person, undaunted by her past and its despairs. But Zackarias discovers another self behind her mask of social adjustment: "She had not faith in anyone or anything. The world was there and everything went on as before, but she had lost her sense of direction and become a whit for the winds. Without rudder, without a goal, without a future" (61). To illustrate for the reader her true state of mind, he tells her about Hedvig and her son, a grim story of love and rejection of love.

One winter, Hedvig, a woman who does ironing, had loved a sailor who left her in the spring, pregnant, and forever bound by her love for him. Her son, Joel, grew up to be a crippled tyrant; she had dropped him on the floor when he was a baby and he was paralyzed for life. Whenever anyone remarked about her suffering his abuses without complaints she calmly replied, "It was I who dropped him," thus taking upon herself the responsibility for his misery.

Joel "carried his sufferings with hatred" (69). He hates all people
— even his mother who patiently tends to his needs, suffering his
hate in love.

She tries to teach him that everything in life is interdependent,
that people consume each other through constant exchange of services and use of each other's time in work and relationships, down to
even the most trivial matter. She tells him that he too consumes
others' time as they consume his, and this ultimately leads to
equality among people. Hedvig, like Luther and Marx, argues that
work is the only true measure of human value because the time we
put into our work has the same quality regardless of the nature of our
work or the result.

But this perspective on life does not satisfy Joel, who continues to
humiliate her to the point of ordering her out on the streets to bring
home a prostitute for him. Ironically, Joel falls in love with the most
repulsive of these women, is cheated out of his money by her, and
left alone to suffer unrequited love. As the pain now replaces his
hate, Hedvig sees her son finally become human, her equal in their
shared experience of loving and losing their love. The traumatic experience changes Joel's attitude toward self and life, and he "builds
himself a new castle" of work instead of his old one of hate.
Likewise, Zackarias assures Klara, she will be able to build herself a
new castle to replace her lost love.

Zackarias fights his impulse to fall in love with Klara because he
believes that his calling is to express the love of many in his work as a
writer: "Zackarias did not come closer to anyone. Nor was he
brought farther away. He stood always at the same distance. He
wanted to see everything. When it came to himself he preferred
however to be silent . . ." (95); "He told stories but he told other
people's stories" (96). But he has promised to help Klara find work
and a place to stay. Therefore, they spend many days together, and
Klara showers him with caresses which he receives with mixed feelings:

Her caresses however arouse a strange pain in him and sometimes when she
looked into his eyes a certain way they were filled with tears against his will.

This made him ashamed. In spite of his inquisitiveness he did not really
want to know whence the pain and the tears. (129)

In this predicament Zackarias does not dare to be alone with
Klara, but takes her out to meet people and, we understand from the
people they meet, to find intellectual stimulus to balance his growing emotional attachment to Klara.

They run into Zackarias' father and Alexis Bring, a journalist and philosopher who lecture them on the nature of art and literature. To further detach himself from the enticement Klara offers, Zackarias tells her another story, which illustrates his own feelings of being many people in one body, and yet being destined to a life of loneliness.

Shortly thereafter they join a group which is going to help Paulina challenge a regulation on store signs which threatens the rights of her friend Fredriksson. This is the first time Klara meets Jan-Alf, Paulina's illegitimate son, whom she will soon love. To foreshadow their future love, Fredriksson tells a story of the eternal novelty of love.

There was once, he says, a Christian people called the "virginites." They claimed that the world meets man anew each morning and that the world is always new for each person. The world's and God's mysterious future did not frighten them (179). Then there was another people called the "sun worshippers." They believed in a cosmic cycle which repeats itself; this gave them a sense of security and assured them of eternity. To them the virginites' belief in a constantly new world was a threat to order and permanence and therefore a dangerous credo which would lead to chaos.

The virginites were persecuted and killed in masses, but a few thousand managed to escape and found refuge where they could continue their way of life. They believed that "Everything is new because everything is placed in time and space" (182). To each person, his birth as well as his death is new to him and therefore not placed in cyclical order. They shared everything in complete equality: "They did not put a price on work according to a scale. . . . All work is necessary, they said, how can it then be given different value?" (182).

Though the world was always virginal to them, they did not ask virginity of each other. Just as their world was new each day because the previous day was never to return, each person's past was of no concern in the present when a man and a woman united in love of each other.

The story anticipates Klara's and Jan-Alf's love, of which they themselves are as yet unaware, and it tells that in each person love finds something untouched by social reality and therefore valuable in itself.

When Klara notices that Jan-Alf is looking at her, she asks Zackarias about his family. Jan-Alf was born seven months after

Leopold's return from a four years' search for social dignity. Paulina had explained that Jan-Alf was prematurely born and although Leopold had never let her know that he did not believe her, he constantly tormented the boy and rejected his advances. The lack of communication with Leopold had made Jan-Alf miserable and he had found happiness only in music: "Each time he could reexperience the beautiful mystery of a single note receiving life by finding its context and its special place among the different notes" (191). Music seen as relationships between notes, which though different together create a uniform whole, stands as an inspiration for a creation of human relationships, Jan-Alf thinks. But Leopold does not understand him and persists in alienating himself from Jan-Alf.

Still Jan-Alf loves him and when he learns that Leopold may have committed a burglary he takes Leopold's crime upon himself and is put in jail. But he escapes to get a chance to declare his love for Klara before he serves his sentence.

As the market days roll on and Leopold does not return, Paulina's worry and longing for him grow. Ahlin expresses her psychological condition, as he often does, in terms of physical movement and domestic work: she walks back and forth pressing her hands together whispering, "My beloved body" (262), thinking about how she had physically enjoyed her pregnancies, thinking about all the tables she has set, beds made, laundry done, life processes that had passed through her hands and body, constantly changing form and yet remaining the same. Time consumed and yet new time to consume. She walks through the streets thinking about Leopold, trying to blend her mind with his, to think his thoughts. She passes Alexis Bring without seeing him, but the meeting evokes a vision in him, a desire to return to the womb, sinking into her arms and shrinking to the size of a child, a longing reminding us of the clown's dream in Bergman's *The Naked Night* produced a few years earlier.

Undisturbed, Paulina continues her way. She thinks about love:

She lived therein [the creation of love] and was someone surrounded by it. Love does not change the nature of the lovers. The happy love performs a completely new act when it arises in two people and unites them in its form. . . . Within its form rules other than those from outside prevail. . . . The important matter is not what you share but that you share. . . .
. . . The whole time she had been prepared to live with him, regardless of how he changed regardless of what he had to share with her. But he had left her. He had refused to offer to share his inadequacy. . . . He dreamed of all

goodness in their union and through the dream he became an enemy to the life therein. (283)

Suddenly she stops wondering what she is doing and is struck by an insatiable craving for hardtack with extra salt butter and chopped chives. Food in Ahlin's work not only carries sensual connotations, it also serves as an escape from distress.

The market is nearly over, and Paulina still has not found Leopold, though he has been seen in town. Yet in her distress she arranges for Jan-Alf to meet Klara so that he may tell her about his love. Deciding to share her future with Jan-Alf, Klara wants to meet his father. Therefore, Zackarias and Klara take the train to meet Merry-Frasse *(Glada-Frasse)*, Jan-Alf's real father, a clown full of songs, jokes, and strings of nonsense words, seemingly incapable of saying or doing anything serious. But Zackarias tells Klara that he has not always been so. He has lead a varied life, first as a logger, then as a railroad worker and a tourist guide. But he could not hide his talent for the comic and the grotesque which made him act, he thought, as if he were a stranger to himself.

Merry-Frasse's coming to town means that the market days are approaching their climax. Paulina, exhausted by work, sits on her bed, her mind wandering first to the fire then to a vision of Leopold riding toward her on a runaway horse which he manages to master. As she is about to turn off the light, Leopold enters the room.

He smiles. He undresses slowly and she notices his clean clothes and body, realizing that he wants her to notice them and to understand their significance: he has returned as a new man cleansed from the shame of his failures. Coming to bed, he begins to touch her; she receives his caresses with joy, though she believes that her fatigue will prevent her from responding fully to him. But he continues to caress her patiently, knowingly, until at last they are able to enjoy each other fully. Afterward Leopold is hungry and as he eats lustfully in the kitchen he tells her that he has now become the man he thinks she deserves.

Returning from Stockholm a few days ago, he had learned that the German counsel has financial troubles. Leopold had suggested that the counsel set fire to his villa, to let a few unpleasant papers burn, and at the same time cash in on his insurance. For a fee, Leopold had offered to devise an "accidental" way to start the fire, but had insisted that the counsel himself light it.

Paulina listens to the account of his crime with disapproval and

sorrow which he fails to perceive because of his childish pleasure at
being able to shower her with money he himself has procured. Finally he feels that he is worth something in his own eyes. But Paulina
wants him to go to the police after the market days when she can join
him and share his punishment.

Then follows an inner monologue by Paulina about life, death,
and love, the biological nature of womanhood, and her "doomsmood" which gives her the courage to confess the truth about the
fatherhood of Jan-Alf. Her guilt, like Leopold's, is part of her life
and cannot be escaped: "Leopold I can never reject you. . . . I am
your lover. If your existence is unconsecrated I will still reach you
there and consecrate you with my death" (406). But Leopold does
not admit to his guilt and therefore she feels that he should die.
Before she is to kill him she seeks moral support from Alexis Bring.
She finds him in his apartment dressed in several layers of clothing,
cold though it is warm. She walks around restlessly and finally asks,
"May one murder, Alexis?" (412) whereupon he plunges into a long
philosophical discourse about the irrelevance of the impersonal
"one" to individual destiny and action. In a stream of examples,
Alexis Bring tells her that generalizations and ideals are not reliable
instruments for guiding the individual in his particular circum-
stances.

Paulina listens intensely to his rapid succession of references to
language, culture, philosophy, religion, and literature, mingled with
examples from Alexis' own experience and people he has met. The
verbosity of his answer provides an ironic contrast to her simply formulated questions: "May one murder?" "How do you get rid of
your heart and how do you get it back unharmed?" (421). But he
sums it all up in a short statement: "Paulina, no situation repeats any
other situation. Then how will any authority be able to deliver you
from your questions of conscience and liberate you from personal
responsibility?" (424).

Alexis Bring continues his rambling discourse, whose words
Paulina cannot follow. Instead she feels their meaning intuitively
through his voice and intonations. Nor is it easy for the reader to
grasp fully all the connotations of his speech, with its multitude of
examples and literary allusions, ridiculing, condemning, and exposing man's need for ideals and guidelines. His speech culminates in a
discourse on Kierkegaard's treatise of subjectivity and the concept of
the individual. Just as Alexis refuses to give Paulina the answer she
seeks, so does Ahlin refuse to give his reader what he wants: "truths"
and illusions neatly wrapped up in coherent narrative.[27]

Paulina listens to Alexis' incessantly flowing speech: she, all body, and he, all intellect, each representing an extreme form of humanness, together form a complex human being; separately they represent female and male principles, emotion and intellect.

Alexis Bring speaks about himself and language in terms reminiscent of the young Zackarias: "I believed that I mapped out reality with the help of all the words; they were a way to keep from losing oneself in this reality or even to come in contact with it" (438). Alexis Bring is a lover of observation, of analytical, intellectual life; but, he implies, his life is not "real" life.

But to be something, no matter what, and that only and nothing else is an ideal. In the world of reality we are all sorts of things and that we are simultaneously. It is in the language and only in the language you can make radical juxtapositions and put good and evil, right and wrong, beautiful and ugly, pure and impure opposite each other, in ourselves all this is brought together and inseparable, because we are organic creatures." (439)

No philosophy, religion, or dogma can help man in his individual dilemma, Alexis Bring says, because they offer a one-sided view of reality, though it is proclaimed to be the true and only reality.

Paulina finally decides that she must kill Leopold, to "consecrate him with death," because he has turned love into a business commodity which can be bought with money or rank. He has also made crime less of a shame than to receive love undeservedly. His value system is perverted by his social will and Paulina cannot permit this socially warped consciousness of his to continue living.

As she carries out her decision, night descends over the marketplace. During the celebrations of the end of the Market, Paulina asks Zackarias' father to help her pull a cart with Leopold's body. Zackarias helps them to lift the dead Leopold onto the cart and, when his father and Paulina leave, his insides stiffen and freeze, and he runs in panic back to the marketplace, where he finds the big doll costume he had been dressed in only a few hours earlier in a mood of gaiety and play. With the doll in his arms, he feels calmer and sits down in the tent where Jan-Alf and Klara have declared their love for each other. Here Jan-Alf had found his place in life, and had therefore decided to give himself up to the police and take his punishment.

There seems to be a place for everyone, a place which makes them feel confident about their future even though it may bring punishment and hardship. The exception is Zackarias who feels he belongs nowhere and to no one. He puts on the doll costume, climbs from the tent, and starts walking back and forth — finally able to weep inside the doll's head — while he beats its face from inside with his fists.

I have no audible genitive[28] he cried — and now. . . . Now he could smile and cry at the same time, but he did not know if it was from irony, happiness, or plain exasperation he smiled and cried. It is night for me he continued therefore. It is night in my market tent. But . . . your task is to honor man, no matter what happens, Alexis' voice fluttered in his head. (460)

In this mood he meets Kornelius Fält who is also alone. He and Zackarias go home together and Zackarias suddenly falls asleep at his kitchen whereupon Kornelius carries him to a bed. As he puts him down, Zackarias squints and thinks while looking at him: "I am lost. . . . I can only play games, there is no seriousness in me. I am rejected, one who stands outside" (461), and a few minutes later again he cries with a smile on his lips.

B   *The writer as lover*

In one of his essays Ahlin defines his role of writer as being like "an impersonal lover,"[29] meaning that he wishes to relate to his characters intensely but without personal and emotional involvement. His characters, he claims, do not reflect his individual qualities but represent general aspects of the human condition and embody universal, rather than unique qualities. Therefore, he calls himself also an "identifier,"[30] someone who represents many different people with equal compassion, whether they are good or bad, successes or failures.

Ahlin found a literary model for this artistic attitude in André Gide's *The Counterfeiters*, whose implied author and narrator presents similar views on the relationship between the writer and his characters, views also formulated by Gide in his *Journal to the Counterfeiters*. By his insistence that the writer should not be confused with his characters, Ahlin also rebelled against the subjective or autobiographical novel which had long dominated Swedish literature. This tradition reached its peak during the 1930s, the decade during which Ahlin studied and tried to become a writer.[31]

By being an impersonal lover, the writer indicates that his love is not directed to one particular person, but to many. Young Zackarias, who is to become a writer, must therefore be on guard against Klara's charm; he cannot devote his life to her alone:

. . . he must protect himself. . . . She threatened him. Dangerous words lie on his tongue. . . . To be able to say in earnest "I love you." . . . The words, he felt, would change him. Did he want that? No, I am not like others. . . . Zackarias was not closer to any one person. . . . He always stood at the same distance. He wanted to see everything and be able to speak about everything. (95)

Just as he was afraid, in the beginning of *The Great Amnesia*, of growing up, realizing that life entails suffering, he is afraid now to commit himself in love which, he has learned from Klara's stories, also brings suffering.

Zackarias wants to tell other people's stories, he says in *Night in the Market Tent*, in words echoing Ahlin's own from an essay: "I wanted from the beginning to become a writer of epics, a portrayer of other people's existence."[32] And to prepare himself for this, Zackarias "listens to other people" (108), observes, and tells stories. Zackarias' night in the market tent is, as Hans-Göran Ekman points out in "Humor och ironi i Natt i marknadstältet" ("Humor and Irony in *Night in the Market Tent*"), the same kind of night described by C. J. L. Almquist in "Skaldens natt" ("The Night of the Poet"), symbolizing the poet's necessary detachment from his work. He creates "playfully," like a child, unconcerned about the facts of reality. Ultimately, however, the poet in Almquist finds his isolation from life unbearable.[33]

Zackarias, too, finds that even in the role of observer, he is not free from despair and suffering. Having helped his father and Paulina load Leopold's dead body onto a cart, he runs out, incapable emotionally and intellectually of understanding what has lead Paulina to kill her husband. "His feelings thought that anything could happen to anybody — except for him; nothing happened to him even if great distress lay ahead. . . . He was outside all happenings, he was a cursed outsider" (455). Inside the big doll's head he could cry, a sign that he was, after all, not cursed to remain outside life as an observer. This was a sign, but not a conviction:

Aunt [Paulina], he thought, do I cry like you? Were the tears an affirmation of and love for the changeable, varying, enigmatic life, the never ceasing stream constantly giving and taking, creating and destroying, giving life and consuming life. And how could he smile with these tears in his eyes? It is night here, he whispered, hitting the monstrous forehead of the doll. It is night in the world's market tent. (460)

Tears belong to a life of love to Paulina, whose life is totally
fashioned by love, making it possible to cry *and* smile. At the very
end of the novel, Zackarias too can cry and smile at the same time.
This indicates that he shares Paulina's humoristic attitude to life: he
can feel sorrow and joy at the same time, an attitude which is necessary for relating to others with love.

Although we can see Zackarias, like most of Ahlin's other young
boys, as the writer's alter ego, he is not the only one who represents
views we can trace back to Ahlin's personal writings. Alexis Bring,
with his intellectual approach to art, complements Zackarias'
capacity for compassion and empathy; since all three qualities are
equally important in creating art, Alexis' exclusive intellectualism is
not creative. It is a life-negating quality which is expressed symbolically by his physical isolation from his environment, by the
layers of clothing he needs to keep warm. Warmth in Ahlin's work
often stands for emotional qualities and these Alexis Bring lacks; he
is always cold, he cannot cry.

In his speeches to Zackarias and Paulina about art, Alexis Bring
sounds much like Ahlin. Alexis claims that naturalism is not a valid
art form today, a thesis which resounds throughout Ahlin's
theoretical work from his early essays to his later radio speeches.[34] In
naturalism, Ahlin argues through Alexis, there is not enough formal
detachment between the artist and his work. There the artist deals
with the quality of life when he should concern himself with the
quality of art:

I say that naturalism is art. It is just not desirable art. It derides man. Not
because it portrays man as crude, evil, disgusting. Dear God, man is all bad
things too. . . . No, but because not even the naturalistic artist can refrain
from putting himself above his subject. Good art is vital, powerful, sensible,
all good that man has. An artist cannot seriously imitate life's changes
between good and bad. That would threaten the high quality of art. (146)

Alexis means here that in order to be able to portray man with the
respect and dignity he deserves, even in degrading and lowly conditions, the artist must stand emotionally free from his motif. The consequence of this freedom, or detachment, is that the writer must not
be in love with "himself," that is, his power of emotional persuasion,
but treat his subject with love. This means that he must refrain from
affecting his readers emotionally so that the reader will forget his
own existence or take sides for or against good or bad characters.

In his aesthetics, Alexis too brings to his work the idea of the writer as lover. But his own love is undelivered and trapped in his complete incapacity to relate physically to others. And yet in a sense he relates to Paulina, as much a lover as Leopold. When Paulina comes to him in agony over her dilemma about whether or not she should kill Leopold, her mind is as exhausted as her body had been when Leopold returned home. She receives Alexis' shower of words as if she were receiving the caresses of a lover, trying to respond, to relate, to share. Her attitude becomes apparent in her use of the same words to Alexis as she had said to Leopold earlier: "Oh, you must work so hard with me."

Both men do at last release her from fatigue or indecision, but with the opposite results. While Leopold brings her back to the invigorating love they shared their first years together, Alexis brings her to decide that Leopold must die. The bipolar qualities of existence: life and death, love and negation of love, acceptance of life and escape from life, are here expressed in the relationship between man and woman, which, as Birgitta Trotzig observes, "shows that the extremes are dependent on each other for their existence."[35] This notion that extreme qualities define each other, that, for example, the "high" qualities are high only in comparison with the "low" ones, forms a theme throughout all of Ahlin's work. It lies at the heart of his message that equality is a necessity of life which is expressed in the union of extremes, in the form of a new existence taking place in love and death.

X   Normal Course

A   *The plot: Love on trial*

With its few characters and comparatively simple plot, *Gilla gång (Normal Course*, 1958)[36] is a chamber play in comparison to the preceding *Night in the Market Tent*. The novel deals with the relationship of an elderly couple, Lage and Berta, who work as school janitors. Berta also works as a highly respected cook at a fashionable summer restaurant. Normally they have enjoyed each other, enjoyed life's little pleasures, but recently Berta has begun to feel old and worthless for no apparent reason; Lage loves her and cherishes her as much as always.

Complications between them begin to emerge in the form of disagreements about how to deal with their daughter Maria. They also feel alienated toward their son, a school inspector, because his letters are full of words they cannot understand. They must go to the principal's office at night to consult a dictionary to decipher his communications.

Lage is one of Ahlin's few sensual male characters. He relates to life humorously, accepting its high and low qualities. He likes to spend time during the summer with his handmade row boats; he enjoys looking at their form, touching the wood, knowing that he has built them. One day while he is standing by his boats, a man, Isak, approaches him.

Isak is looking for Maria, with whom he has been living for several months in the little village where she is a schoolteacher. She has left him for no apparent reason, and this hurts Isak's male pride. Lage and Isak both represent virility, but in opposing ways. While Lage's virility is a function of his emotional authority and his tenderness toward all things, Isak seems more like an untamed animal. He has "animal eyes" and conveys a sense of emotional brutality. Lage, who dislikes him instantly, refuses to help him find Maria.

Lage hopes that after her experience with a bad man, Maria will become interested in Göran, an unpretentious man who has withdrawn from all personal relations to atone for his accidental killing of a schoolmate when he was only a boy. Although Berta, along with the community, looks upon Göran as a killer, Lage respects him and believes him capable of loving and caring for others, once he is brought out of his self-imposed emotional isolation.

Lage soon learns that Maria is hiding at Göran's place. She believes that she is pregnant, but is not yet sure and therefore spends her days passively waiting for nature to reveal her true condition. Before she receives an answer she is in limbo. When Berta learns of Maria's suspicions, she wants Maria to have an abortion because she regards social reputation as more important than a child. Lage, however, looks upon pregnancies as sacred events and becomes so upset about Berta's attitude that he strikes her.

He immediately regrets his action, and to atone for his "crime" he leaves the house, removes himself from an environment of love, and goes on a drinking bout. After several days he returns and hides in the basement where Berta finds him. There they speak about their lives and about the meaning of love.

Although they seemingly continue their life as before, Lage misses the feeling of love in himself which he killed when he hit Berta. But in the end the pieces of his life fall into place: Göran and Maria have decided to get married and he can again approach Berta with love. His reawakening is consecrated by a beautiful sexual act:

The night was dark and warm. They were lying on the ground talking to each other as they used to. Now Lage experienced that he again could reach Berta. He was allowed to and could lie next to her body and he came into it as before.

This was a big moment he had ceased to hope for. When he first noticed her "shelter" opened to him, he did not dare to believe it. Nothing had changed, it seemed. And yet the "restraints" that used to surround him were gone. It felt as if he had thrown off a heavy burden. Again he could reach her beloved face with his lips. Life trembled in him. The moment was shimmering like the dark surface of the sea. Afterward he understood that he was promised continuation. Life would take its normal course as before. (324)

B *Love tested, love regained*

The all-pervading need for and power of love was conveyed structurally in *Night in the Market Tent* through the multiplicity of human destinies projecting many aspects of man and of love. In *Normal Course,* the verbal structure in the form of neologistic word formations symbolizes how love creates its own forms of existence, free from established meanings or evaluations. And yet, the new words are not totally separated from a social foundation because they are built upon established conventions for word formation. But Lage infuses them with new meanings by changing their forms and thereby indicating that extraordinary meanings, and by analogy people's qualities, exist together with the apparent form created by social conventions. We need only a new perspective on the old form to discover its hidden qualities. Love will provide us with this perspective, but we must be willing to see ourselves and others through the eyes of love.

Lage, who meets life with love, contributes most of the new word formations in the novel. This is an indication of his capacity to look at life with fresh eyes, unprejudiced by norms or by society's judgments. This becomes particularly evident in his attitude toward Göran. It saddens Lage to see the young man denying himself what is good in life: togetherness, human relations, and love. In Lage's words, Göran decided "to reject himself" *(att förkasta sig)* to demonstrate his moral guilt for the killing of his classmate. The verb itself belongs to standard vocabulary, but its reflexive form is not standard grammar. Here the form illustrates its special connotation of an act directed inward by the subject:

Lage knew something about the peculiar element coloring Göran's life. . . . There are people who at some time in their lives have rejected themselves. . . . They are the opposites of the "demanders," those who, standing in the midst of the life always cry: I have not gotten my share. . . .

Those who have rejected themselves feel, just because they have chosen to reject themselves, that they are in their right places, where they ought to be. . . . They carry their guilt in their hands, having made it into a candle. It was the candle that lead them to reject themselves. . . . And they reject themselves away from the good in life. . . . They have always rejected themselves from something normal . . . : no woman for me, no, no children for me, no — keep away from all togetherness, from all intimate relations. (131 - 32)

Each time the chance for a normal life arises, the rejection must be repeated; the first time Lage tries to take Göran out of his self-rejection by suggesting that Maria needs him, Göran is not willing to listen to him. However, when Maria herself seeks shelter with Göran, he discovers that he too can love and be loved. They soon decide to get married and Lage marvels at the change in Göran, brought about by Maria:

To me it is something great that has happened between you. You see Maria, he had rejected himself. He was capable of that. But you took him out of his choice of rejection. It is a marvel to have witnessed such a thing. . . .

Of course the two of you did it, not you alone. But by himself Göran would never have abandoned his own rejection. (318)

The transformation in Göran occurred when Maria came to him alone, detached from the rest of the world. Since he had rejected only his relationship with the world but not rejected anybody in particular, his attitude becomes irrelevant when he is confronted with one person apart from the rest of the world. Maria is different; she is divorced from the world because of her personal situation, and therefore she emerges as a single face from a world with a multitude of faces, a world which is in a personal sense faceless. With Maria, Göran's world ceases to be impersonal and becomes person-related. This helps him accept love in spite of his guilt.

From the beginning Lage seems perfectly at peace with the world which he relates to through unconditional love, demonstrated particularly in his relationship with Göran. But his notion of love is tested when he is driven to act in disagreement with his concept of self. When he strikes Berta, he violates the principle of love and is crushed by feelings of guilt. Paradoxically, his love has forced him to act against his own feelings of love: though he loves Berta, he violates her dignity in order to defend his idea of the absolute dignity of life.

In this situation he thinks that he should, like Göran, reject himself and leave the good life with Berta. But he returns to Berta, humble in his realization that he is not capable of any grandiose gestures of despair: ". . . he had nothing great to display in front of doors and windows. No choice of rejection, no decision of deep despair . . ." (289). Therefore, he is not a great man, he thinks. He cannot even give Berta the magnificent gesture of rejecting her love.

He tries to explain his feelings to Berta who at first does not understand:

I wanted to reject myself.
What was that? Reject. . . . What do you mean?
I wanted to reject myself away from you. (311)

He says that he should have stayed away from her from the beginning of their relationship, but that he had been too weak to make such a big decision. In other words, Lage also believes that good things in life must be earned, or at least that *he* must earn his good life. Though he gives his love unconditionally, he cannot receive love with the same attitude.

Up to this point, Berta has been portrayed as a strong-willed woman. She is well aware of her social worth as the best cook in town and as an efficient supervisor of the school's crew of cleaning women, but lately she has come to doubt her worth to Lage. However, when Lage confesses his feelings of his own unworthiness, she argues against the notion that any form of unworthiness can exist in a relationship based on love, thereby denouncing the validity of her doubts about herself.

She suggests they sit in judgment of each other; she has "doomsmood," and points out to Lage that he, by wanting to decide about the future of their relationship without consulting her, violated the very basis for a true relationship of love. Nothing but their love for each other should be important in their judgment of each other.

But Lage still feels he is too much of a failure to be able to relate to Berta in mutual love. As he tells Maria, "I have been sustained by my love for your mother and by her love. This is no longer so. Love no longer reaches me. It is hopelessly crushed by my present mood *(det som nu passar på mig)*. It feels like a disease in me and that is probably what it is, too" (320). Then, at the end, love unexpectedly returns to his life, and he is able to recapture the essence of their earlier relationship and to love Berta as before. This is expressed in terms of the poetic experience of regained sexual bliss. Although nothing has changed, love has come to him spontaneously, "unmotivated," like a gift from God. Now he understands truly that love is unconcerned with merit: "Many years from then, he thought with gratitude about his life in this world, how happily, how blessedly good it had been. That in his case things had turned out so well was not by any merit of his he knew and he pointed that out on appropriate occasions" (324). The novel ends here, more conclusively than do most of Ahlin's novels.

XI Bark and Leaves

A *The plot: Toward a commitment of love*

Bark och löv (Bark and Leaves, 1961)[37] is a novel about art and love. The title alludes to the myth about Apollo and the nymph Daphne, who became a tree in order to escape his pursuit. In this myth, Kai Henmark argues, we find an image of how love is incapable of conquering the guards and removing the disguises hiding the beloved one. It can also be read as an image of the artist's difficulty in being understood and received by his audience.[38] First we meet the writer Erik who is in love with the painter Aino. She has been living with Erik periodically after having left her husband Sivert, a film director (who bears some resemblance to Ingmar Bergman). Erik wishes she would commit herself totally to him, would "die into" *(dö in i)* him. When his emotional demands become too threatening to her as an artist and an individual, she takes refuge with George, another writer. She wants to give Erik only her "surface" *(yta)*.

Erik tells about his recent visit with Sivert when he had been driven by Sivert's valet-driver, Hudu. At this point Erik digresses into a long monologue about Hudu's function in Sivert's films and Sivert's problem with his critics. The monologue carries over into a discussion about the relation between art and reality, and while he is involved with this problem, Aino rings the doorbell.

Before he opens the door he conjures up a setting from his past: a cottage where he could have gone to find the solitude he needs were it not for the fact that his stepmother lives close by. She constitutes a disturbing element in his life because he is too emotionally attached to her. Just as she is still alive within him, Sivert is alive inside Aino, and this prevents them from creating something out of their present lives.

Sivert too has a person inside him who appears in his dreams. He dreams about making love and suddenly discovers that the woman is shaped like a bottle which, he sees to his horror, contains a man. This appalls him because he thinks the dream means that there is a woman inside him too. It frightens him because he believes such an intimate relationship with a woman would destroy his creativity.

The next chapter is the first of Erik's two recollections from his youth, which take the form of stories independent of the main plot. They seem at first to deal with another person: a boy or young man called Mats or Mats Olof. First we meet Mats who is living with an eighty-year-old woman, Lotten, and helping her prepare and serve coffee to the dockworkers. Mats is filled with what he calls his "thirst" which saved him from depression. Mats' "thirst" was aroused when he became aware of his need to love one woman. Lotten, who has spent her whole life in loving and caring for many people, disapproves of his one-sided view on love. Love, she believes, is accomplished in relation to all people one meets in life.

But we come to understand that their views are not completely different after all. Mats had, after a period of alienation from the world, suddenly discovered that the meaning of the commandment that man shall love his neighbor is that he shall love himself:

My unloved neighbor was no one but myself. I was unloved *(ungeliebt)*. I was my own enemy. With this insight I had found my neighbor and I began to love him. . . . The unloved became loved. Then my thirst was born. And thanks to the thirst I realized that the woman to whom I will be united, is living somewhere among people. . . . An unloved woman is living for me. Where is she? I want to make her loved. She needs me as I need her. We will taste each other's lives. We will commit the acts of love with each other. My union with her will also be my union with the world. (89)

And Lotten prays he will find his unloved woman.

This digression into Erik's past is followed by a chapter containing a monologue by Aino, who represents a principle of artistic attitude rather than a psychologically conceived character. She discusses her past in relation to her present impotence as an artist: art had become her life and she had believed that her art would be able to preserve and convey the passion she felt when she created it. She was relating to her creations with sensual pleasure; each work became an intercourse. When she realized that her audience did not respond to her art with the same feelings she had felt when she created it, she had lost her impetus to create. The lack of communication between her and her audience had made both art and existence lose their mean-

ing, and she does not see how she will ever regain her confidence as
an artist and as a human being. She asks Erik to liberate her from her
predicament, using almost the same phrase he had used when he
defined his conception of an ideal relationship with her. She says: "I
want to die into my image (*Jag vill dö in i min bild*)" (131).

The chapter following her monologue is titled "Invitation to:
dying into one's image," and illustrates the lack of viability in
aesthetics which claim that art should be an imitation of nature.
Erik, here portrayed as the fifteen-year-old Mats Olof, meets Anders
Bläda, his mother's rejected lover. At Mats Olof's mother's wedding,
Anders had been the traditional "wedding bear" wrapped in a bear
skin and symbolically killed to transfer his power to the groom.

Anders thinks longingly about the moment when he and the bear
were one entity, one "image," and he pleads with Mats Olof to command him to unite with the flesh and hide of an animal, just as his
mother's eyes had ordered him to become the "wedding bear." At
first Anders Bläda frightens Mats Olof, but when Anders sends him
money and his address he decides to go to the forest where Anders
and his sister Elizabeth live. When Mats Olof meets Anders Bläda
the second time, he is no longer frightened by him. They spend
some time in a cabin where Anders talks primarily about the nature
of the moose. Mats Olof soon realizes that the moose has become
Anders' image of himself, but he does not understand the implica-
tion of this until Anders shoots a moose, cuts it open, crawls inside
and shoots himself.

When Mats Olof finds Anders dead inside the animal, he understands why Anders died this way, but he is distraught because he
cannot comprehend any harmony or oneness between the dead man
and his image, the moose. Later Elizabeth tells him that the man
and his image did merge into one idea. She also tells him that he
must learn to live his own life, and she repeats Anders Bläda's words
to him, that he must find his harmony according to his own ideals
and not seek to conform to other's ideals.

The experiences with Anders and Elizabeth make Mats aware of a
power within himself which he calls "joy." He realizes that all that
we love and embrace with joy can be taken from us and leave us with
a longing we can never overcome. He finds it hard to accept life with
these conditions, but then he remembers the street car cleaning
woman, Svea, who had been deprived of love her whole life. She had
transferred her longing for personal love into grief, an equally strong
emotional power, and thus had been able to continue her life

without love while retaining the energy of love. Shortly after meeting with Svea, Mats Olof finds something which can relate to his feeling of "joy," namely books. "But," the chapter ends, "out in life, as it were, experiences with many kinds of people were waiting for him" (249).

In the last chapter Erik resumes his discussion of his relationship with Aino, begun in the first chapter. She is now living with George because she is afraid that her relationship with Erik was going to turn into love and demand an unbearably heavy sense of commitment from her. She keeps calling Erik, however, and speaks about George's work; at the same time George seems to be talking to Erik about art. It is difficult to distinguish between the voices which seem to run together into a monologue.

One day George leaves Aino after having been writing furiously for days and nights, and she then wants to return to Erik. She does not yet know whether she will be able to live with him and love him, but she wants to try. Now it is Erik who is unproductive, and he receives her with his back toward her. She begins to caress him, using the same gestures which Elizabeth used with Mats Olof after Anders Bläda's death. As she caresses him she whispers, "You . . . ," indicating that she is ready to abandon her "I" and unite with him, to let him under her surface. They seem to be approaching the beginning of a new relationship which carries the seed of ultimate commitment, and Erik feels stirring within him new ways of living and writing, generated by their love: "I felt that our relationship had become, at the same time, simpler and more difficult. I experienced already the initial movements from a new language" (330).

B *To love oneself outside oneself*

His experience as Mats and Mats Olof have taught Erik that his life is not complete without love. Aino, however, confuses art with life and thinks that her life is not complete if she cannot function as an artist. While Erik believes that love will enhance creativity, Aino sees art as a substitute for love and refuses to believe that she can be an artist and a lover at the same time. Preferring to be an artist, she rejects love, because she says: "To love is to die" (252). Since she thinks that art is equal to life, that is, self, to die, that is, to give of herself totally in love, would mean to die as an artist.

Her attitude is ultimately self-defeating. Unable to communicate through art, she tries to compensate for this lost power through sex. But sex divorced from love, we recall from earlier novels, becomes a frantic and empty experience, not a comforting and creative one. Erik, who believes that art is a form of love, continues to write and remains in a sense creative, although he has not yet found a new form of communication and therefore writes "dead letters" *(döda brev)*. He needs Aino to love and give him love, because only then will he acquire a new language, the *"viva vox"* he now lacks.

Aino illustrates the despair of an artist who finds that her artistic attitude has become invalid. She is used to identifying emotionally with the reality she paints: "Earlier, while I was still 'standing up' there was always an interplay between my world and myself. I imagined I was the one who created the emotional climate and extracted its seasons from canvas and paint" (99). Then, when her aesthetic principles no longer serve to put "life" into her work, she feels alienated and becomes passive: "I hated, Erik. I was in darkness. My aesthetic dogmatism of the old order was hanging in the museums. The dogma alone had given bones to the meat, goal and purpose to the paint. Now everything fell apart and continues to do so" (109).

Therefore she begs Erik to help her find her place in the world again: "Make me simple, Mats Erik. Help me to say: My death is my own" (110); ". . . I want to disappear. I want to die into my image. Help me Erik. Save me this way" (131). But Erik does not want to help her this way because he loves her. He wants her to accept the fact that life offers no simple solutions for its sufferings and that art is not an imitation of life in the world. Nor is the task of today's artist simple; he must find a new way to communicate with his audience, and there are no guidelines for him to follow.

Traditionally the artist "died into his image," Ahlin argues through Erik's and Aino's discussions about art and reality, art and the artist, art and the audience. The artist's emotions were conveyed to the audience through his power of emotional persuasion, which swept the audience off its feet and carried it into a world created by the artist. He presented an imitation of life and concealed his own role as a creator of this world of fiction in order not to disturb his audience's suspension of disbelief which, ideally, was the reception he was striving for.

Today, however, the artist's dream of presenting "life" in his art by, paradoxically, "dying into" it, no longer serves a purpose. The creative motive behind the new novel must be "love" instead of "life." Love is realized in a dialogue between the reader and the writer. This dialogue takes place in the final ordering of the text into a meaningful work. The relationships between words, ideas, and characters on the one hand, and style, structure of time and space, point of view and characterization on the other, are ultimately established by each reader as he understands them from his level of experience and insight.

This means that the artist must love himself outside himself, but not, as Alexis Bring tells Zackarias in *Night in the Market Tent*, by putting himself above his motif and making his world emotionally intrude into the reader's world. To become creative again, Aino must, by analogy, learn to love herself outside herself by committing herself to Erik in love. "Die into me," he pleads, "stricken by your love for me, die in the midst of your life's heart, yield, dare" (286).

He knows that only love can save them from their barren existence, uncreative and unloved by their audience. When he first began to love himself, he began to love his neighbor, because he then understood how to fulfill his neighbor's need for love. Therefore he believes that as he and Aino love each other, they also love the other in themselves. This love will enable them to create and to communicate with their audience again because they will, through love, understand the needs to fulfill in others.

But as long as Aino wants to die into her own image, to return to the tradition that has proven sterile, she cannot love, nor can art become a creative function in her. She has no sense of worth outside this tradition, and she does not believe in love as a creative energy. Only when she learns not to put herself above her motif, and instead to change her pronoun from "my" image to "your" image, will she be able to love and, it is implied, to create.

This happens at the very end. Aino has arrived at Erik's place and he thinks: "She was an image and I saw myself as an image. And she gave birth to her image before my eyes" (329). Shortly thereafter Aino begins to caress him and whisper: "Erik-Mats-Olof-George-Cleve and all the rest you turn yourself into; now we are here. . . . Then she whispered: 'You . . .'" (330). The pronouns are here very important for the meaning. The "you," "we," "you" apparently refer to both Erik and herself, and this, together with the indication that Erik in fact represents most of the other characters of the novel, shows that Aino, by sharing his identities, is willing to share his life. Sharing is love. Love is work. Work is creation. They now stand in a mutual "I"-"Thou" relationship based on love, and the dead language of convention will be replaced by the living language of love.

CHAPTER 7

The Short Stories

AHLIN'S short stories have been highly praised, even by those critics who had received his novels with some reservations. Most of the short stories are published in three collections, *Inga ögon väntar mig* (*No Eyes Await Me*, 1944), *Fångnas glädje* (*Joy of the Imprisoned*, 1947), and *Huset har ingen filial* (*The House Has No Annex*, 1949). Others are published in journals and newspapers. Though some of these uncollected stories are of great interest, for example, "Hemliga manipulationer" ("Secret Manipulations"),[1] one of Ahlin's earliest stories, this discussion will be confined to examples from the three collections.

In his short stories, Ahlin deals with the same problems he discusses in the novels: man's entrapment in his own feelings of inadequacy, man's only comfort in this world being human relations and yet his inability to create such relations, and how this sense of social failure keeps man from loving himself and others. Critics have been impressed by how clearly and concisely Ahlin has presented in the short stories the same topics reviewers had had difficulty digesting in the novels, with their greater verbiage and their greater demand on reader attention.

Structurally, the short stories conform to the literary ideals of their time, namely, the "new American prose," represented by the behavioristic school of literature, Hemingway and his followers. Ironically, while Ahlin vehemently rejected the nineteenth-century naturalism as a valid literary form for his novels, he adopted what he himself calls "a new artful version of naturalism" for his short stories. But at the same time, he questions the tenability of this new literary style.[2]

The stories in the first collection, *No Eyes Await Me*, illustrate the Pauline saying: "I do not understand what I am doing, for I do not do what I want to do; I do things that I hate. I can will but I cannot do what is right. . . . I do not do the good things that I want to do; I do the wrong things that I do not want to do" (Rom. 7:15 - 19). Lennart Göthberg, in an insightful review of Ahlin's work, argues that the stories illustrate Luther's thesis about man's enslaved will.[3] Among other places, Luther developed this thesis in his "The Bondage of the Will" and in *Lectures on Romans*.

In the first story, "Coming Home to Be Nice," we meet a worker coming home drunk Saturday evening, trying to appease his wife with a bag of fruit, but unable to tell her that he is sorry. He wants her to understand that though he did give in to the temptation to get drunk, he did after all come home in the evening instead of spending the night drinking with his friends and whatever women they might pick up. She is unhappy because she cannot love him unconditionally; instead of greeting him with a smile and a warm embrace as she wants to, she sits down to peel potatoes. As the despair of their inability to communicate their inner feelings grows in each of them, he keeps repeating that he came home to be nice and she continues to peel potatoes: "She looked down into the bowl at the thin, dirt-grey, meandering peels. Suddenly she thought there was a brain, a human brain, or perhaps God's brain, lying there in the bowl in her lap."[4]

This idea fills her with an existential despair and now, psychologically transferred outside her personal situation, she manages to bring herself to approach her husband. She throws her arms around him and asks him to help her because she is so afraid. Her gesture serves to release him emotionally: "He was so ashamed that he could neither swallow nor breathe" (15). He feels unworthy to touch her, but she leads him to the couch where they lie down, pressed closely together.

They know that nothing has really changed and that the same scene will be repeated, but this knowledge no longer keeps them apart. "On the contrary, it made them taste each other more deeply and completely" (16). This, Göthberg says, "is genuine Lutheran psychology which teaches about the evil and unchangeable heart of man, whose chains first begin to break when he becomes conscious of his sin and guilt." The story is a masterpiece and probably the most widely known text by Ahlin. In 1969 it was turned into a highly successful television drama.

The title story, "No Eyes Await Me" is another skillfully composed story. It tells of an unloved and therefore nonexisting man who sits emotionally isolated from his family, who busy themselves around him as if he were not there. They never look into his eyes;

they relate to him only on the surface. This story illustrates another Pauline inspired thesis: to see is to love, and consequently, to love is to see. This is brought out at the end of St. Paul's famous Epistle to the Corinthians where he defines love and describes the time when love will govern the world: "For now we are looking at a dim reflection in a mirror, but then we shall see face to face" (1 Cor. 13:12). The notion of seeing being an aspect of love is also mentioned in such a classical theological tract as Ludwig Feuerbach's *The Essence of Christianity:* "To see is a divine act. Happiness lies in mere sight of the beloved one. The glance is the certainty of love."[5]

Man's spiritual weakness and his inability to predict the effect of his actions, which may be contrary to his will, is illustrated in "The Wonderful Night Gown." The mother of an adolescent girl who is going to play the angel in a Sunday school play insists that she wear the mother's luxurious nightgown for the part. Less interested in her daughter's appearance than in seducing the young Salvation Army Sunday schoolteacher, the mother uses her provocative nightgown on her innocent daughter to get her way. In this story, Göthberg comments, Ahlin tells us that "nobody is so good that he cannot be the worst, that not even an angel can protect herself from causing the fall of other people."

Loneliness and the ever-unsatisfied need for togetherness form the central theme in the stories of *Joy of the Imprisoned.* Here man is presented as pitifully unable to communicate or to relate to others, and yet the characters retain a form of dignity in their pitifulness. Paradoxically, the characters seem to command more respect the more they reveal their weaknesses and degradation. Ahlin achieves this effect because, in the process of exposing his characters' pathetic nature, he creates in the reader a sense of identification with the human condition. The strength it takes to admit to one's weakness turns pitifulness into dignity.

This is true of the crippled woman in "Kvinnan och döden" ("The Woman and Death"), who is used and trampled upon by different men during her pathetic search for love, until she gives in to a long felt yearning and limps into a river. The story was made into a short film by Gösta Werner in 1965 with the title "Väntande vatten" ("Waiting Waters").[6]

The divorced father in the title story is used by his child. The boy's exploitation of his father's need for love contrasts powerfully with the father's undisguised demonstration of his need for emotional contact. In "Squeezed" we get one of Ahlin's many masterful portrayals of female psychology. Mother and daughter meet covertly in an outhouse so as not to anger the daughter's husband who does not want them to see each other. He is impotent and unable to relate emotionally to his wife. But he caresses his skis like a lover as he spreads tar on their bottoms. The daughter's love for her husband is unshakeable, although he rejects all her attempts for physical or any other form of contact. This makes the mother feel infinitely sad because she thinks her daughter is worthy of a better life. At the same time she understands that her daughter's love for her husband, however unmerited, must not be questioned. The story comments beautifully on man's limited power for solving the injustices he sees around him. This, Ahlin suggests, can only be done in a spiritual sense, by God; our social injustices are inescapable.

That human love is not in itself sufficient to save man from despair forms the theme of the stories in *The House Has No Annex*. In the title story, the childless woman artist, now uncreative, tries to persuade the French boy who was her "war child" during World War II to come back to her and become her son permanently. But she learns that love cannot be acquired, only given, and that loneliness is a human invention. If man had faith in God, love would become a matter of life itself. Only when she accepts her loneliness is she filled with a sense of togetherness, and as she waves goodbye to the boy she feels her creative powers return.

CHAPTER 8

Equality — A Conclusion

THE special connotations of love and death in Ahlin's work have been widely discussed, although they have not been comprehensively examined against a theological background as is done in the present analysis.[1] Furthermore, the conceptual relationship between love, death, and equality, though noted by other critics, has not been explored throughout Ahlin's major productions.[2] The theme of equality, and its related motifs, so consistently employed and explored by Ahlin, are particularly important in view of the impact his writings have had upon the literary and cultural consciousness of modern Sweden.

Ahlin views equality as man's birthright which society has defiled by introducing hierarchies of merit, and by implanting in him the need to strive for higher social status and recognition. By pointing at this destructive element in society, Ahlin stands as one of the important contributors to the development of a philosophy of man suitable for the ideals of the contemporary Swedish welfare state. Younger critics in particular have focused upon the social message inherent in his theological frame of reference.

Leif Zern sums up the relationship between love and equality in the following words: "The model for equality is love and if his characters finally arrive at a sense of equality, this happens because they have stepped out of the *game of merits (värdespelet)*."[3] Through love social merits and rewards become *adiaphora* because, as Anna Boëthius says, "in a relationship of love there no longer exists a conflict between man's concept of self and his concept of the world outside self." And she couples love with death in a series of definitions putting an equal sign between them in terms of their effect on man: love and death both "find man," (outside value systems), "set man's [spiritual] wealth free," and "liberate man."[4]

Man is freed by love and death to "relate to a person in his

144

totality," Nielsen argues. He continues, "All that Ahlin says about equality must be understood in the context of love and death." The liberation found in death or love "rejects the idea that a person can qualify or disqualify himself conclusively."[5] Qualifications are made by society, and, as Saga Oscarsson points out in "The Theme of Equality in *Night in the Market Tent*," "Society's ordinary system of evaluation is a threat to a fundamental community of love and work."[6]

Equality in work is achieved only if man honors his work apart from its social context and status. Man is, however, not conditioned to do so; instead, he compares the status value of his work to others' work value, and feels inferior if he does not measure up to the standard he had been striving for. Work should, however, be appreciated as an output of unqualified energy; making man's status, instead of his expended energy, an index of his social worth is destructive. Thus Paulina, in *Night in the Market Tent*, deplores in a philosophical soliloquy by her kitchen table: "She valued her work and knew its importance. Therefore her self was nourished by her work. . . . And she wanted it to be so for everyone. The work must not be silent. It must resound. One's self needs the importance of work or it will become impoverished and regard life with contempt."[7] This is easier for women to accomplish, she believes, because their work is more immediately related to life. But it is not easy for men. They hunt for honor, for a higher rank, they must push each other down to raise themselves up socially. This makes it impossible for them to live:

This damages love. I know that from my own experience. Suddenly I learned that love itself was subject to destruction although the world was standing there as before. Work cannot mean anything to them, well, then love must also become unimportant. No, at once it becomes forbidden to love. An utter misfit cannot love, they say now. . . . They reject the whole world if they cannot produce a flower to adorn their beloved.[8]

The notion that work defines a man's worth is also refuted by Erik's discussion of equality in *Bark and Leaves:* "If equality does not exist we must invent it," he says in an often quoted line. Shortly after this statement, he continues, "it is work that awaits us; not the realization of ideals. . . . This has nothing to do with our worth. . . . Here and now worth and work and the result of work are mixed and interlaced. This is why equality must be invented and it must be constantly renewed."[9]

This means that each time man is confronted with a system, a scale, a spiral of ever-raising expectations[10] which will not leave him at peace with himself, he must reaffirm his faith in the principle of equality and reject any notion that he can as a person be labeled, weighed, and priced. He can be so judged as a janitor, a baker, a construction worker, or a salesman, but he cannot relate to his death or his love which define his equality, except from his personal locus (*ort*) in the world. In this place he is not identical to anyone else and cannot be compared to anyone else. Free from comparisons, he is also free from degradations, superlatives, and feelings of inferiority. He can accept his life with its misery *and* its ecstacy without reservation.

We have seen how Ahlin, through his work, developed these concepts, interweaving them as if he were composing a fugue, letting one concept at times dominate the others, but never losing any one of them. Thus woven into an impressive and engaging body of work, he has shown us the complexity of life in a message of few words: equality exists in love, work, and death. These are the great three, and the greatest of them is love.

Notes and References

Chapter One

1. Biographical facts when not otherwise indicated are taken from Erik Hjalmar Linder, *Ny Illustrerad Svensk Litteraturhistoria. Fem decennier av nittonhundratalet* (Stockholm: Natur och Kultur, 1966), pp. 912 - 46, and Lars Furuland, "Lars Ahlin — ursprungsmiljö och bildningsgång," in *Synpunkter på Lars Ahlin*, ed. Lars Furuland (Stockholm: Aldus/Bonniers, 1971), pp. 9 - 42.

2. Interview in *Morgontidningen*, October 1, 1957.

3. Birger Lundberg, "Resandegrabben som blev en känd författare," *Arbetet*, January 5, 1945.

4. Ivar Öhman later became editor of *Folket i Bild* and is now Sweden's ambassador to Greece.

5. "Möte med Lars Ahlin och hans texter," interview and reportage in Swedish Television, ed. Tone Bengtsson, December 1, 1969. On private tape from the broadcast.

6. "Luther came to a fresh understanding of the Gospel sometime between 1513 and 1519. The most dramatic event in that reconception is generally known as the 'tower experience,' because his new insight apparently came to him when in the tower of the Augustinian monastery in Wittenberg. But exactly when this experience took place and what its precise meaning was are not settled." *Martin Luther. Selections from his writings*, ed. John Dillenberger (New York: Anchor Books, 1961), p. xvii.

7. "Möte med Lars Ahlin och hans texter."

8. Linder, pp. 916 - 17.

9. Lars Ahlin, "In på benet," *Bonniers Litterära Magasin* 39, no. 1 (1970), 9.

10. Conversation with the author, May 24, 1974. See also "Möte med Lars Ahlin och hans texter."

11. Lars Ahlin, "Reflexioner och utkast," in *Kritiskt 40-tal*, ed. Karl Vennberg and Werner Aspenström (Stockholm: Bonniers, 1948), p. 31.

12. See Lars Ahlin's introduction to *Tåbb med manifestet* (Stockholm: Folket i Bilds förlag, 1954). See also "På kvalbänken," *BMF. Organ för*

Svenska Bokhandelsmedhjälpareföreningen 26, no. 10 (December, 1944), 1 - 2, and Furuland, p. 23.

13. Furuland, p. 38.

14. Gunde Fredriksson, "Vreden och nåden. Studier i luthersk teologi och Lars Ahlins 40-tals produktion med särskild hänsyn till dödsmotivet och med beaktande av dramerna Lekpaus och Eld av eld" (Licentiat thesis, University of Stockholm, 1971), p. 214.

15. Furuland, p. 30

16. Lundberg.

17. Ahlin, Introduction to *Tåbb med Manifestet*, p. 6.

18. Ibid.

19. "Den arbetslöses vittnesmål," *Vi* 31, no. 4 (1944), 16.

20. Lars Ahlin, "Om ordkonstens kris," in *Kritiskt 40-tal*, p. 13.

21. Artur Lundkvist, "Ovanlig ansats," *Stockholms-Tidningen,* October 8, 1945.

22. Erik Lindegren, "Lars Ahlins nya roman," *Skogsindustriarbetaren,* no. 22 (1945), 11.

23. Stig Ahlgren, "Quo Vadis, Lars Ahlin?" *Aftontidningen,* October 6, 1945.

24. Sven Stolpe, "Min död är min," *Aftonbladet,* October 4, 1945.

25. Margit Abenius, "Idéroman on människans värdighet," *Bonniers Litterära Magasin* 14, no. 9 (1945), 768 - 71. Pointed out in a letter from Ahlin to the author, June 12, 1975.

26. In *Bonniers Litterära Magasin* 29 (1960), 464 - 75.

27. "Filmglimtar," *Svenska Dagbladet,* July 3, 1949; Anders H. Ångström, "Lars Ahlins film som kom bort, och Erik Lindegrens," *Expressen,* February 15, 1971.

28. Anders H. Ångström, "Porträtt av unga dramatiker: Lars Ahlin," *Teatern* 17, no. 1 (1950), 11 - 12.

29. "Lars Ahlin och Fromma mord," in Erik Hjalmar Linder, *Guds Pennfäktare och andra essäer* (Stockholm: Natur och Kultur, 1955), p. 185.

30. *Vi*, nos. 50 - 51 (1954), 34.

31. Interview in *Morgontidningen,* October 1, 1957.

32. Lars Ahlin, "Ett brev," *Bonniers Litterära Magasin* 29, no. 6 (1960), 476 - 77.

33. "Om ordkonstens kris" was first published in *40-tal*, no. 1 (1945); "Reflexioner och utkast" was first published in *40-tal*, no. 10 (1945); "Konstnärliga arbetsmetoder" was first published in *40-tal*, no. 4 (1947). The essays are also printed in *Kritiskt 40-tal*, pp. 9 - 57.

34. For further discussion of these concepts see Torborg Lundell, "Lars Ahlin's Concept of the Writer as Identificator and Förbedjare," *Scandinavica* 14, no. 1 (1975), 27 - 35.

35. Lars Ahlin, "Att överskrida utan att överge," *Bonniers Litterära Magasin* 34, no. 6 (1965).

36. Furuland, p. 33.

37. Erich Auerbach, *Mimesis* (Princeton: Princeton University Press, 1953), p. 41.

38. Hans-Göran Ekman, *Humor, grotesk och pikaresk. Studier i Lars Ahlin realism* (Östervåla & Uppsala: Bo Cavefors Bokförlag, 1975).

39. Ahlin, "Om ordkonstens kris."

40. Lars Ahlin, "Öppen mot läsaren," broadcast on Swedish Radio, December 28, 1961. An abbreviated version of a speech held at a writer's conference at Biskops-Arnö the same year. See also a summary of this speech in Lars Gustafsson and Lars Bäckström, *Nio brev om romanen* (Stockholm: Bonniers, 1961), pp. 47 - 53.

41. Ahlin, "Om ordkonstens kris," p. 11.

42. Ahlin, "Öppen mot läsaren."

43. Henri Poincaré, *Science and Hypothesis* (1905; reprint ed., N.p.: Dover, 1952).

44. Arne Melberg, *På väg från realismen. En studie i Lars Ahlins författarskap, dess sociala och litterära förutsättningar* (N.p.: Gidlunds, 1973).

45. Melberg, p. 108.

46. Lars Ahlin, "Hemliga manipulationer," *40-tal*, no. 1 (1944).

47. Lars Ahlin, "Den berusade båten," *Bonniers Litterära Magasin* 30, no. 4 (1961), 282.

48. Melberg, pp. 110 - 15.

49. "Filmglimtar."

50. Ingmar Bergman, *Bergman on Bergman*, interviews by Stig Björkman, Torsten Manns, Jonas Sima, trans. Paul Britten Austin (London: Secker & Warburg, 1973), p. 13.

51. Ahlin, "Den berusade båten," and "Att överskrida utan att överge."

52. Ahlin, "Öppen mot läsaren," "Denna världen vår," broadcast on Swedish Radio, May 25, 1966; "Fakta och fikta," broadcast on Swedish Radio, June 1, 1966; "Sex punkter om Paulus," broadcast on Swedish Radio, June 8, 1966; "Därför skriver jag," interview by Carl-Magnus von Seth and introduction by Erik Hjalmar Linder, broadcast on Swedish Radio, September 7, 1968.

Chapter Two

1. Lars Ahlin, *Tåbb med manifestet* (1943; reprint ed., Stockholm: Folket i Bilds förlag, 1954). Quotes in the text are followed by page number referring to this edition.

2. Lumpenproletarian, according to Marx, is a person who lacks social consciousness and sees to his own fortune before he considers what is good for society. Among the lumpenproletarians Marx lists: ". . . decayed *roués* with doubtful means of subsistence and of doubtful origin, alongside ruined and adventurous offshots of the bourgeoisie . . . vagabonds, discharged soldiers, discharged jail-birds, escaped galley-slaves, swindlers . . . gamblers . . . brothel-keepers . . . *literati* . . . beggars, in short the whole indifferent

disintegrated mass thrown hither and thither which the French term la Bohème . . ." Karl Marx, "Society of December 10, 1849," in *The Marx-Engels Reader*, ed. Robert C. Tucker (New York: W. W. Norton, 1972), p. 479.

3. Erik Lindegren, "Den arbetslöses vittnesmål," *Vi* 31, no. 4 (1944).

4. Sören Kierkegaard, *Concluding Unscientific Postscript*, trans. David F. Swenson (Princeton: Princeton University Press, 1941), p. 390.

5. Håkan Lantz, "En teologisk läsning av Lars Ahlins Tåbb med manifestet," in *Föreningen lärare i religionskunskap. Årsbok*, vol. 2, ed. Bengt-Erik Benktson, (Lund: Gleerup, 1969), p. 91.

6. Erik A. Nielsen, *Lars Ahlin. Studier i sex romaner*, trans. Jan Gehlin (Stockholm: Bonniers, 1968), p. 91.

7. Carin Lagergård, "Läsa Lars Ahlin med utgångspunkt från ett kapitel ur Bark och löv," mimeographed (Stockholm: St. Lukasstiftelsen, 1970), p. 25.

8. Kai Henmark, *En fågel av eld. Essäer om dikt och engagemang* (Stockholm: Rabén & Sjögren, 1962), pp. 154 - 55.

9. Fredriksson, p. 168.

10. Alrik Gustafson, *A History of Swedish Literature* (Minneapolis: University of Minnesota Press, 1961), p. 455.

11. Lennart Göthberg, "På väg mot en ny klassicism," in *Kritiskt 40-tal*, ed. Karl Vennberg and Werner Aspenström (Stockholm: Bonniers, 1948), p. 168.

12. Nielsen, p. 25.

13. *The Man without a Way*, trans. Leif Sjöberg and Ronald Bates, *New Directions* 21 (1969), 1 - 28.

14. Melberg, p. 145.

15. Ibid., p. 185.

16. Ibid., p. 207.

17. Hans-Göran Ekman, "Humor och ironi i Natt i marknadstältet," in *Synpunkter på Lars Ahlin*, ed. Lars Furuland (Stockholm: Aldus/Bonniers, 1971), p. 123.

18. Ibid., p. 137.

19. Nielsen, p. 147.

20. See Nathan Söderblom, *Humor och melankoli och andra lutherstudier* (Stockholm: Sveriges Kristliga Studentrörelses förlag, 1919), p. 4.

21. Ekman, *Humor, grotesk och pikaresk*.

22. See, for example, Gunnar D. Hansson, "Den dubbla tillhörigheten: En tolkning av Lars Ahlins humoruppfattning," *Tidskrift för litteraturvetenskap* 1, no. 2 (1971 - 1972), 102.

23. See Söderblom, p. 62.

Chapter Three

1. For a discussion of death and failure see also Fredriksson.

2. Martin Luther, *Lectures on Romans*, in *Luther's Works*, ed. Hilton C. Oswald, vol. 25 (Saint Louis: Concordia Publishing House, 1972), p. 310.

3. Ibid., p. 312.

4. Karl Barth, *The Epistle to the Romans*, trans. Edwyn C. Hoskyns (1933; London: Oxford University Press, 1965), p. 209.

5. Ibid., p. 164.

6. Anders Nygren, *Commentary on Romans*, trans. Carl C. Rasmussen (1944; London: SCM Press, 1952), p. 268.

7. Ibid., p. 333.

8. Barth, p. 209.

9. Ibid., p. 194.

10. Karl Marx, "Toward the Critique of Hegel's Philosophy of Law: Introduction," in *Writings of the Young Marx on Philosophy and Society*, trans. and ed. Loyd D. Easton and Kurt H. Guddat (New York: Anchor Books, 1967), p. 263.

11. Ekman.

12. Lars Ahlin, "Reflexioner och utkast," in *Kritiskt 40-tal*, ed. Karl Vennberg and Werner Aspenström (Stockholm: Bonniers, 1948), p. 19.

13. Lars Ahlin, *Min död är min* (1945; reprint ed., Stockholm: Bonniers, 1962). Quotes in the text are given with page numbers referring to this edition.

14. Sten Selander, "Min död är min," *Svenska Dagbladet*, October 4, 1945.

15. Birgitta Trotzig, "Till de levandes lov," *Bonniers Litterära Magasin* 34, no. 4 (1965), 244.

16. Lars Ahlin, "Den ringastes like," in *Bekännare och förnekare*, ed. Alan Fagerström (Stockholm: Bonniers, 1950), p. 37.

17. Anders Nygren, *Eros och Agape* (1930; reprint ed., Stockholm: Verbum, 1966), p. 537.

18. See Fredriksson, p. 159.

19. See Melberg, p. 174.

20. See Nielsen, p. 45.

21. See Lars Ahlin, "Reflexioner och utkast," in *Kritiskt 40-tal*, pp. 18 - 19.

22. Lennart Göthberg in *Den nya Parnassen*, ed. Gustaf Näsström (Stockholm: Norstedt, 1947), p. 13.

23. See also a comparison between the two dwarfs in Ekman, pp. 162 - 66.

24. Nielsen, p. 33; Ekman, p. 162.

25. Nielsen, pp. 33 - 34.

26. Ekman, p. 196.

27. *Stockholms-Tidningen*, August 3, 1953.

28. See Nielsen, p. 109.

29. Interview in *Dagens Nyheter*, August 28, 1952.

30. Ingmar Bergman, *Four Screenplays*, trans. Lars Malmström and David Kushner (New York: Simon & Schuster, 1960), p. 152.

31. Örjan Wallquist, "Kommentar till Fromma mord," *Arbetet*, February 18, 1953.

32. Nielsen, pp. 88 - 89.

33. Melberg, p. 242.

34. Lars Ahlin, *Fromma mord,* 2nd. ed. (Stockholm: Tiden, 1952). Quotes in the text are given with page numbers referring to this edition.

35. Nielsen, p. 98.

36. Paul Tillich, *Love, Power and Justice* (1954; reprint ed., New York: Oxford University Press, 1974), p. 60.

37. See Melberg, p. 243.

38. Ibid.

39. Nielsen, p. 128.

40. Ibid., p. 96.

41. Ibid., p. 105.

42. Lars Ahlin, *Kanelbiten* (1953; reprint ed., Stockholm: Tiden, 1961). Quotes in the text are given with page number referring to this edition.

43. About the wrath of love see Gustaf Aulén, *Den kristna gudsbilden genom seklerna och i nutiden* (1927; reprint ed., Uppsala: Svenska Diakonistyrelsens förlag, 1941), p. 199 - 204.

44. "Nu bränns det för Lars Ahlin," *Vi* 41, nos. 50 - 51 (1954).

45. "Flickan och ensamheten," *Aftonbladet,* November 7, 1953.

46. "Den utvaldas ensamhet," *Svenska Dagbladet,* November 7, 1953.

Chapter Four

1. Lars Ahlin, *Om* (1946; reprint ed., Stockholm: Bonniers, 1958). Quotes in the text are given with page numbers referring to this edition.

2. For further discussion see Torborg Lundell, "Lars Ahlin's Concept of the Writer as Identificator and Förbedjare," *Scandinavica* 14, no. 1 (1975), 27 - 35.

3. Ulf Linde, "Det Ahlinska alternativet," *Bonniers Litterära Magasin* 29, no. 6 (1960), 468.

4. Nielsen, p. 78.

5. Linde, p. 472.

6. Nielsen, p. 57.

7. Linde, p. 472.

8. Ibid., p. 474.

9. Fyodor Dostoevski, *The Brothers Karamazov* (New York: Random House, 1950), p. 301.

10. Nielsen, p. 76.

11. Lars Ahlin, *Jungfrun i det gröna* (1947; reprint ed., Stockholm: Bonniers, 1964). Quotes in the text are given with page numbers referring to this edition. The title is the name of a flower whose Latin name, *Nigella Damascena,* has been chosen for the English title, because a direct translation of its Swedish name, the virgin in the grass, would be misleading. The characteristics of the flower are significant for our understanding of the female protagonist who is said to carry within her an image of the flower. It is described by Ahlin to be so strangely shaped that its pistils are far too tall for its stamen to reach. Not until the last moment, when the flower seems

destined to die unfertilized, will the pistils "conquer their feminine inhibitions" (30) and bend backward until they touch the stamen thus creating life in the moment of death.
12. Melberg, p. 211.
13. Lars Ahlin, *Egen spis* (1948; reprint Stockholm: Tiden, 1953). Quotes in the text are given with page numbers referring to this edition.

Chapter Five

1. Lars Ahlin, *Stora glömskan* (1954; reprint ed., Stockholm: Delfin/ Bonniers, 1964). Quotes in the text are given with page numbers referring to this edition.
2. See Gustaf Wingren, *Luthers lära om kallelsen*, 3rd. ed. (1942; reprint ed., Malmö: Gleerup, 1960), p. 78.
3. See Wingren, p. 31.
4. Letter from the author November 14, 1975.
5. Gustaf Aulén, *Den kristna gudsbilden genom seklerna och i nutiden* (Stockholm: Svenska Kyrkans Diakonistyrelses förlag, 1941), p. 198.
6. Until 1955 Swedes were allowed to buy liquor only in limited quantities rationed per month. In restaurants one was allowed to drink a limited quantity per person and liquor could only be ordered with food.
7. Sigmund Freud, *The Interpretation of Dreams*, trans. and ed. James Strachey (New York: Avon Books, 1968); reprint of volumes 4 and 5 of the standard edition (London: Hogarth Press, 1953), p. 363.
8. Freud, p. 355.
9. Örjan Lindberger, "Nu bränns det för Lars Ahlin," *Vi* 41, nos. 50 - 51 (1954), 34.
10. Gunnar Brandell, "Stora erinringen," *Svenska Dagbladet*, October 8, 1954.

Chapter Six

1. Furuland, p. 37.
2. Anders Nygren, *Eros och Agape* (1930; reprint ed., Stockholm: Verbum, 1966), abridged version in two volumes, p. 54.
3. Martin Luther, *Lectures on Romans*, in *Luther's Works*, vol. 25, ed. Hilton C. Oswald (Saint Louis: Concordia Publishing House, 1971), p. 294.
4. Nygren, pp. 54 - 57.
5. Ibid., p. 72.
6. Ibid., p. 73.
7. Ibid., p. 79.
8. See also Aulén, p. 199.
9. Nygren, p. 110.
10. Ibid., p. 617.

11. Luther, p. 512; see also Gustaf Wingren, *Luthers lära om kallelsen*, 3rd. ed. (1942; reprint ed., Malmö: Gleerup, 1960), p. 23.

12. Ibid., p. 227.

13. Dietrich Bonhoeffer, *Ethics* (1949; reprint ed., New York: Macmillan, 1972), p. 52.

14. Luther, p. 512.

15. Ibid., p. 378.

16. Ibid.

17. *The Complete Bible*, trans. Edgar J. Goodspeed (Chicago: University of Chicago Press, 1939).

18. See, for example, Lars Ahlin, "Den ringastes like," in *Bekännare och förnekare;* Lars Ahlin, "Allt är tillåtet," *Dagens Nyheter*, February 12, 1966; Lars Ahlin, "Världen är en övergående historia," three speeches on Swedish Radio, May 25, June 1, and June 8, 1966.

19. See Fredriksson, who traces Wingren's general influence on Ahlin primarily from Wingren's thesis on Irenaeus. For a discussion on love, *Luthers lära om kallelsen* seems to be a more likely source.

20. Wingren, p. 23.

21. Ibid., p. 57.

22. Lars Ahlin, *Kvinna kvinna* (1955; reprint ed., Stockholm: Bonniers, 1957). Quotes in the text are given with page numbers referring to this edition.

23. Artur Lundkvist, "Berättad folkvisa," *Morgontidningen*, October 1, 1955.

24. Lars Ahlin, *Natt i marknadstältet* (1957; reprint ed., Stockholm: Delfin/ Bonniers, 1960). Quotes in the text are given with page numbers referring to this edition.

25. Nielsen, p. 155.

26. See Hans-Göran Ekman, "Humor och ironi i Natt i marknadstältet," in *Synpunkter på Lars Ahlin*, pp. 122 - 151.

27. Hans-Göran Ekman, "En bok i boken — om Lars Ahlins majevtiska metod," *Komma* 2, no. 3 (1967), 17.

28. In Swedish the genitive ending s is not added to words already ending in s. Zackarias refers to the fact that his name sounds identical in genitive and nominative.

29. Lars Ahlin, "Om ordkonstens kris," in *Kritiskt 40-tal*, p. 10.

30. Torborg Lundell, "Lars Ahlin's Concept of the Writer as Identificator and Förbedjare," *Scandinavica* 14, no. 1 (1975), 27 - 35.

31. Lars Ahlin, "Reflexioner och utkast," in *Kritiskt 40-tal*, p. 15.

32. Ahlin, "Om ordkonstens kris," p. 11.

33. Ekman, "Humor och ironi i Natt i marknadstältet," p. 131.

34. See, for example, Ahlin, "Om ordkonstens kris"; "Konstnärliga arbetsmetoder," in *Kritiskt 40-tal;* "Öppen mot läsaren," program on Swedish Radio, December 28, 1961.

35. Birgitta Trotzig, "Mellan ord och tystnad," *Bonniers Litterära Magasin* 26, no. 8 (1975), 719.

36. Lars Ahlin, *Gilla gång* (Stockholm: Bonniers, 1958). Quotes in the text are given with page numbers referring to this edition.

37. Lars Ahlin, *Bark och löv* (Stockholm: Bonniers, 1961). Quotes in the text are given with page numbers referring to this edition.

38. Kai Henmark, *Jämlikheten och samtalet* (Stockholm: Rabén & Sjögren, 1970), p. 70.

Chapter Seven

1. Lars Ahlin, "Hemliga manipulationer," *40-tal*, no. 1 (1944).
2. Lars Ahlin, "Om ordkonstens kris," in *Kritiskt 40-tal*, p. 14.
3. Lennart Göthberg, "Den trälbundna viljan och den gömda gåvan," *Svenska Morgonbladet*, October 3, 1944.
4. Lars Ahlin, "Kommer hem och är snäll," in *Inga ögon väntar mig* (Stockholm: Tiden, 1944), p. 15. Quotes in the text are given with page numbers referring to this edition.
5. Ludwig Feuerbach, *The Essence of Christianity* (1841; reprint ed., New York: Harper Torchbooks, 1957), p. 56.
6. Gösta Werner, *Den svenska filmens historia. En översikt* (Stockholm: PAN/ Norstedts, 1970), p. 136.

Chapter Eight

1. Gunde Fredriksson's Licentiat thesis "Vreden och nåden" (University of Stockholm, 1971) contains an excellent discussion of the theological background to Ahlin's work of the 1940s. Unfortunately it is unpublished. Other works have discussed individual novels from a theological point of view. See, for example, Håkan Lantz, "En teologisk läsning av Lars Ahlins Tåbb med manifestet," in *Föreningen Lärare i Religionskunskap. Årsbok*, vol. 2, ed. Bengt-Erik Benktsson (Lund: Gleerup, 1969), pp. 87 - 103. A more general discussion of Christian elements in Ahlins work is provided in Olof Hartman, *Jordbävningen i Lissabon* (Stockholm: Rabén & Sjögren, 1968), pp. 112 - 25.
2. For a longer discussion on equality see Torborg Lundell, "Lars Ahlin's Concept of Equality," *Scandinavian Studies* 47, no. 3 (1975), 339 - 51.
3. Leif Zern, "En sörja på gott och ont," *Stockholms-Tidningen*, February 27, 1966.
4. Anna Boëthius, "Ensamhet och gemenskap i Natt i marknadstältet," in *Synpunkter på Lars Ahlin*, pp. 111 - 14.
5. Nielsen, p. 219.

6. Saga Oscarsson, "Jämlikhetstemat i Natt i marknadstältet," in *Synpunkter på Lars Ahlin*, p. 74.

7. Lars Ahlin, *Natt i marknadstältet* (1957; reprint ed., Stockholm: Delfin/ Bonniers, 1960), p. 126.

8. Ahlin, p. 128.

9. Lars Ahlin, *Bark och löv* (Stockholm: Bonniers, 1961), pp. 257 - 8.

10. See Lars Ahlin on "uppskruvningens schema," in "Reflexioner och utkast," in *Kritiskt 40-tal*, p. 31.